Designed by Gillian Greenwood

Knife in the Water
Director Roman Polanski

Roger Manvell

New cinema
in Europe

studio vista|dutton pictureback

General editor David Herbert

Acknowledgements

We owe our thanks to the following distributors and other sources for many of
the stills reproduced: Academy Cinema, Bargate Films, Anglo-Amalgamated,
British Lion, Columbia Pictures, Connoisseur Films, Contemporary Films,
Curzon Film Distributors, Gala Film Distributors, Metro-Goldwyn-Mayer,
Mondial, the National Film Archive, the Rank Organisation, Sebricon, Twentieth-
Century Fox, and Warner-Pathé.

© Roger Manvell 1966
Reprinted 1967, 1970
Published in Great Britain by Studio Vista Limited
Blue Star House, Highgate Hill, London N19
and in the USA by E. P. Dutton and Co Inc
201 Park Avenue South, New York, NY 10003
Set in 8D on 9 pt Univers, 2 pts leaded
Made and printed in Great Britain by
Richard Clay (The Chaucer Press), Ltd, Bungay, Suffolk
SBN: 289 27773 6

Contents

Introduction

This brief account of some of the advances that have been made in post-war feature film-making in Europe is limited to certain countries: Italy, France, Britain, the USSR and Poland. Film-makers working in other countries, for example, Bergman in Sweden, are mentioned individually. This is partly due to the limits of space, and partly to the fact that most of what is really significant in the development of the European cinema is represented by the work of the principal film-makers in these countries.

The main movement of the period has been towards greater naturalism in subjects, characterization and technique, and following this towards a more imaginative understanding of what realism can mean when it is taken beyond mere superficial 'likeness' in the portrayal of people and places. In this sense realism is used here as a term that includes any approach, however extreme, whose final aim is to represent what a film-maker believes to be the truth, or what is real about his subject. It includes, therefore, not only *Saturday Night and Sunday Morning,* obviously, but also Fellini's *8½* and Rivette's *Paris Nous Appartient.*

The cinema has also moved effectively in the direction of presenting symbolism and fable—Bergman's *The Seventh Seal,* for example, and Cocteau's *Orphée.* The symbolic story and the fable are another, equally valid approach to the truth as the artist understands it, though it is not the approach of realism. This movement, small though it has been, is seen most notably of all in certain of the films of Ingmar Bergman.

The reason why the conventional film, which remains the staying power of the cinema as an entertainment industry, is not much mentioned is that it is more concerned with dramatic fantasy than with actuality, or truth. It is the other cinema with which we are primarily concerned—the film which represents some kind of step forward, or step aside from convention.

Whether they have been financially successful or not, most of these films owe their presence on the screen to the fact that there is a film industry to provide their makers with equipment and screen-space. In return for these sometimes rather begrudged favours, the unconventional films help to explore new territories in subjects and characterization, and to develop new techniques.

Recent changes

The past fifteen years have brought interesting changes in the cinema. As an art, the development of the film has always been rapid, largely because it has happened during the twentieth century, in which most changes—social, educational and artistic— have been greatly speeded up.

Because it is a 'popular' art, the cinema both creates and reflects the cultural attitudes of the society it serves. But the cinema can only induce changes in taste that the community, influenced by the cinema and the other forces that are brought to bear simultaneously—publishing, broadcasting and publicity of all kinds—is actually prepared to adopt. Largely because of television, the cinema no longer holds its former unique position as the only popular visual medium. This is evident enough. Yet it still has a considerable influence on popular taste, and sets a standard in many fields, not least through the images created by the stars and the publicity that attends them, and the picture of social behaviour it so vividly presents.

People in most countries, whether these are what are termed developed or under-developed, have never been confronted by such a continuous assault-by-image as they are today, in the 1960s. Few who have continual access to the modern press, television and film even want to resist the effects of this assault; for the most part they try to keep up with what appears to be fashionable in social habits, taste and outlook.

It is largely because of this that the operation of film censorship has changed so radically since the late 1950s. The first major challenge to the British inhibitions represented by the censorship office just after the war came in the field of publishing, with the unsuccessful prosecution of *The Philanderer* for obscenity in 1954, followed by the historic trial in 1960 concerning the appearance in print of the uncut version of *Lady Chatterley's Lover*. In the theatre a similar challenge came with the controversial production of *Look Back in Anger* in 1956. The censors of both drama and film found they were able to alter their sights to a considerable extent, and so reflect the obvious changes that were taking place in public acceptance. Films began to appear on the British screen with both subjects and dialogue that responded to this new, far less inhibited attitude—for example, *Room at the Top* in 1958. A parallel recession in film censorship restriction took

8

place in the United States, and British and American films began to vie with each other in frankness, while in Sweden, for instance, Ingmar Bergman pushed back the limits of Europe's most liberal censorship farther still with the successive challenges he made in films such as *The Virgin Spring* (1959) and *The Silence* (1963).

It is now a full generation since the general public during the 1920s became aware of the work of Freud; the recognition of the significance of irrational experience, and a vague but growing popular acceptance of its importance, has meant that advanced films, like books, could draw increasingly on this great and revealing source of imagery. This began comparatively early in the cinema, particularly in certain of the avant-garde films of the 1920s—the films of Buñuel, for example, and, more self-consciously, in Germaine Dulac's film from Antonin Artaud's script, *The Seashell and the Clergyman,* or, later, in Jean Vigo's *Zéro de Conduite.* Cocteau's esoteric showmanship demonstrated the capacity of the film to weave together the images of actuality and illusion, and so helped to make acceptable to larger audiences after the war the illusory experiences in films such as Fellini's *8½,* Rivette's *Paris Nous Appartient* or Resnais's *L'Année Dernière à Marienbad.* This is a great advance on the well-signposted nightmares and crude symbols of hallucination of the popular cinema— the contrived imagery of the kind Hitchcock created in his psychological thriller *Spellbound.* John Huston even produced *Freud: The Secret Passion* in Europe, a sympathetic and brilliant film which attempted with some success to explain in popular terms the significance of Freud's initial researches.

Another significant change has occurred which affects the economic position occupied by the more advanced forms of film-making. Though films of this kind are still primarily distributed through the specialized cinemas in Britain, or through the art theatres of North America, their influence on the more conventional forms of production has increased considerably. They receive much more attention in the press than was formerly the case, and they enjoy much wider publicity through the innumerable international film festivals that have spread across the world. Also the phenomenal growth of the film society movement in many countries has helped still further to build a conscious (sometimes a self-conscious) public that hastens to admire everything that appears to reflect the latest developments.

Though the conventional cinema still remains stolidly conventional, even it cannot remain for ever unaffected by the work of

9

so many well-publicized directors of the more advanced schools. Furthermore, with the catastrophic decline in North American and European cinema-attendance since television and other social attractions and distractions have claimed their share of the public's attention, the cinemas have needed fresh inducements to bring audiences back to big-screen entertainment. Alongside the great spectaculars (such as *El Cid, Cleopatra* and the Cinerama shows) and the films featuring really sensational stars (Marilyn Monroe, Brigitte Bardot, James Dean or Marlon Brando during their peak fame), have come the films of the independent producers who were determined to make their individual, personal mark in the cinema—producer-directors such as the Americans Otto Preminger (*Anatomy of a Murder, Exodus, Advise and Consent, The Cardinal*), George Stevens (*Shane, Giant, The Greatest Story Ever Told*), Stanley Kubrick (*Spartacus, Lolita, Dr Strangelove*) and the British David Lean (*The Bridge on the River Kwai, Lawrence of Arabia*, both produced by the American, Sam Spiegel). Alongside them have developed the Italian producers, such as Carlo Ponti and Dino de Laurentiis, who pride themselves on sponsoring spectacular and, in the case of de Laurentiis, sensationally unconventional films.

The success of the cinema in the face of television depends increasingly on the flair, showmanship and imagination of such film-makers as these who, either as producers or directors, force the public to take note of their work—which means going to see their films. This, to a considerable extent, accounts for the wide distribution and high reputation of films which, only ten years ago, would either have stayed within a limited, isolated, high-brow market, or would never have been made at all.

In fact, the old, hard-and-fast line of demarcation between the low and middle-brow cinema on the one hand, and the isolated, high-brow cinema on the other, that existed both before and to some extent after the war, has become blurred, though it has by no means disappeared. It still exists more clearly in Britain and the United States than it does in Italy, France, Sweden and Poland. In these continental countries the film-makers who are more adventurous in subject and treatment can still also be popular with the public, although it would be very wrong to suggest that they do not suffer from commercial and censorship difficulties. But all the evidence is on the side of a considerable maturing of the cinema in these countries, with a new range of acceptance developing in the film-going public. In Britain and

America it is at least no longer considered eccentric to be interested in the more unusual kind of film. Tens of thousands of people are sharing these interests everywhere, and the films themselves are widely discussed in print and through broadcasting.

Although the film industry in Britain follows patterns of distribution which are very similar to those of the past—the chains of provincial cinemas alter their programmes regularly, once or sometimes twice a week—there are many signs of change here too, which result from the increasing interdependence of the various larger film-producing countries. With the gradual break-up of the big Hollywood producing-organizations during the 1950s, and the drastic reduction in the quantity of Hollywood's output of staple feature films, on which a large part of the world's cinemas had come to depend, such changes were inevitable. Many of the prominent American independent producers have tended to leave Hollywood to the television series manufacturers, and go abroad in search of new locations, new subjects and cheaper labour. The majority of the European stars, once limited to appearing in films made in their own particular language, have now become familiar

Lawrence of Arabia Britain 1962. Director David Lean
Peter O'Toole

(mostly with dubbed voices) to other nations in the endless succession of co-productions made between Italy, France and Spain, or have reached even wider audiences by starring in English-language films made by American, British and, latterly, Italian producers. Many of the resulting films (good as well as trivial) may seem curiously hybrid in their casting—in *Rocco and his Brothers* that purist director Luchino Visconti was prepared to create a Sicilian working-class family out of a cast made up of Greek, Italian and French stars, while in *The Leopard* he accepted the American Burt Lancaster for the part of a Sicilian patrician, in a production made primarily for the English-language and not the Italian-speaking market. The Italians, in fact, have been making a bold bid to create in Italy a European Hollywood, while Spain, with its considerable and still cheaper film-making resources and even securer sunshine, has been trying to follow this example.

It is always deceptive to talk of a shift in audience taste. Basic interests never really change—people read novels, attend plays or watch them on television, and go to see films because they are fascinated by the spectacle of how other people behave in trouble; the curse is taken off this sometimes morbid curiosity simply because these fictional people are not real, though the naturalism with which they are portrayed by skilful actors and actresses becomes an additional factor in the entertainment. So, apart from farcical comedies and other lighter shows, most films deal, more or less sternly, with people in dire danger or dire distress.

What does change in public taste is the relative degree of sophistication with which these fictional characters can be presented, and the nature of the trouble they are in. The shift during the 1950s and 1960s has been in the direction of greater complexity; both characterization and acting have become on the whole less simplified than formerly, and the psychological and social dilemmas in which the characters are placed are more realistically, even sensationally, treated. While the typical 'problem' films of the mid-1950s were, for example, *Les Jeux Interdits* or *Nous Sommes Tous Des Assassins* in France, or *The Cruel Sea* and *Orders to Kill* in Britain, those of the 1960s have moved on to *La Dolce Vita* in Italy, *Jules et Jim* in France, *Knife in the Water* in Poland, *A Taste of Honey* and *A Kind of Loving* in Britain. These are all films which could be said to belong to the category of accepted entertainment, at least in their own countries. In the more rarefied atmosphere of the 'specialized' film, the social, moral and psychological complications of an *Umberto D, Un Condamné à Mort s'est Echappé, The Seventh Seal* and *Ashes and Diamonds* in the 1950s have been succeeded in the 1960s by those of *The Eclipse, Il Mare, Vivre Sa Vie* or *Paris Nous Appartient.*

The economics of film production have also shifted ground to a limited extent. The principal attraction the film industry offers still remains the star system—the personalities and talents of well-established, well-liked stars are the only points of interest most people recognize in advance about a new film, and the stars normally remain the most reliable means of attracting people into the cinema. But the stars no longer excite the almost slavish following that they used once to do, and still do in the almost isolated case of the 'pop' singer's very temporary hold on the teenage public. Many films are produced now which attract audiences largely because of their subject or their background—how many millions of people went to see *Lawrence of Arabia* because it featured the new star, Peter O'Toole? Very few stars now are able to attract vast audiences in Europe solely by the appearance of their names in a film's advance publicity.

With the virtual elimination of habitual cinema attendance, film-goers now make a deliberate choice of the features they want to see, and they choose them only partly because of the stars appearing in them. This change of emphasis in the public's interest in films has helped the more individual directors to choose subjects well outside the conventional range, and to some extent to use lesser-known players because of their suitability for the principal parts. How else can the production of such films as *Dr Strangelove* be explained? In one way or another such unconventional films have helped to widen the range of what it has become customary for cinema-goers to regard as entertainment. There was a time when a subject had to be immediately recognizable as standard entertainment, or audiences, if they came at all, would walk out during the screening.

It is in stimulating the new interest in subject-matter rather than stars that the more responsible critics play their part. A critic is obviously concerned with the evaluation of a film as a whole—the subject, the story, the treatment in screen terms, the acting. To the critic, stars remain actors giving good, indifferent or bad performances in good, indifferent or bad films. Informed film criticism is read or listened to on the radio by an increasing number of people, and the circulation of the responsible film journals has grown correspondingly. Support of the film society

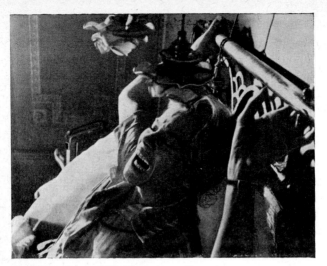

The Silence Sweden 1963. Director Ingmar Bergman
Ingrid Thulin

movement, as we have seen, has developed phenomenally in many countries. The press in various forms has become a means by which hundreds of thousands of readers have acquired some discrimination in their response to the films they see.

A little progress has also been made in the long struggle to create conditions by means of which better films can be produced and distributed. Though it is unlikely that Jean Vigo, were he alive today, would find it any easier to obtain commercial sponsorship for *Zéro de Conduite* than he did in 1933, he might at least begin to find some common ground with an industry capable of making a success of *Les Quatre Cents Coups, The Silence, A Taste of Honey, $8\frac{1}{2}$, Aparajito* or *Viridiana*.

The range of individual film-making, and its successful distribution (on however great or modest a scale) has grown considerably since 1950. It is the purpose of this book to illustrate and discuss briefly some characteristics of this new range of film-making in Europe, and to show more especially how it has developed in Italy, France, Britain, the USSR and Poland, countries in which some advance has been made in recent years.

The movement towards realism

Films have on the whole moved towards a far greater realism. When the older, more conventional American and European films of the 1930s and even later are revived, one is almost always struck by their stagey, studio presentation in comparison with the representation of surface realism in modern films. Everything in the past was subjected to the scriptwriter's and director's desire to make the flow of the plot absolutely clear; films were delivered in well-shaped paragraphs or sequences, while the actors only too often capered through their dialogue like well-drilled, highly professional dummies. The sets had a kind of tidied-up, studio-made appearance, while the outdoor settings looked, and mostly were, artificial. Very few films made in the 1930s escape from this studio-bound appearance.

Most films which have the modern look of actuality about them owed this initially to the war films of the 1940s. It is curious that an event of such inhumanity should have forced us to bring humanity to its representation on the screen. Audiences with some form of direct experience of war demanded, in the treatment of war subjects, an authenticity of a kind more familiar in documentary films than in the studio feature film. This authenticity subsequently spread from war subjects to peace subjects—or at least to crime fiction, notably in America. A few extraordinary films, such as *Citizen Kane* (1941) or *The Magnificent Ambersons* (1942), neither of which were so popular with audiences at the time of their initial release as they were with the critics, or David Lean's realistic handling of Noel Coward's scripts for *This Happy Breed* (1944) and *Brief Encounter* (1945), had already begun to establish the kind of naturalism in treatment and acting that faced audiences with people on the screen who were more or less like themselves.

This was something revolutionary. It is true that audiences had always wanted to 'identify' themselves with the characters on the screen, but largely for reasons of wishful thinking and the desire to escape into a world of unreality. The new films invited them to accept the characters as being like themselves, while in the better films dealing with unusual or highly dramatic experiences the characterization and acting were deliberately drawn as close to life as possible, as in, for example, Carol Reed's films of the immediate post-war period, *Odd Man Out* (1947), *The Fallen Idol* (1948) and *The Third Man* (1949). In the treatment of the story, the harder kind of sequence-divisions or paragraphing of the plot was giving place to the more fluid forms of continuity characteristic of the better films of the later period.

A glance at some of the principal films of 1947–9 shows that the new realism was becoming well-established in Europe and the United States. In America it was mostly associated with crime and gangster films, often now shot freely on location—films such as *Crossfire* and *Boomerang* (both 1947), *Call Northside 777*, *Naked City* and *Act of Violence* (1948), and *They Live by Night*, *The Set-Up* and *All the King's Men* (1949). But America was also bringing a new realism (sometimes over-sensationalized) to the treatment of other subjects—to the rehabilitation of men affected by war service in *The Best Years of Our Lives* (1947) and *Twelve O'Clock High* (1949), to mental illness in *The Snake-Pit* (1948), to race relations in *Intruder in the Dust* (1949), to child welfare in *The Quiet One* (1948). A more fluid kind of technique was introduced by John Huston in his early film *The Treasure of Sierra Madre* (1948), with its striking characters and locations, and its allusive kind of dialogue, the exact significance of which was not always superficially apparent and needed an imaginative participation by the audience.

The new realism was paralleled in Europe, notably in Italy, where the so-called neo-realist movement had already made what seemed at the time an almost miraculous appearance, with Visconti's *Ossessione* (1942, for long unseen outside Italy for copyright reasons), with Rossellini's celebrated *Rome, Open City* (1945) and *Paisa* (1946), and with de Sica's less spectacular but more socially sensitive film *Shoeshine* (1946). These were followed by Visconti's Sicilian film *La Terra Trema* (1948), while in France realism was also apparent in Clément's *La Bataille du Rail* (1945), and was developed further in Claude Autant-Lara's *Le Diable au Corps* (1947). In Poland the first signs of a remarkable talent for exact observation appeared in Wanda Jacobowska's film of Auschwitz, *The Last Stage* (1948), while in Sweden Alf Sjöberg had made *Frenzy* in 1944, and Ingmar Bergman had directed his first, distinctive feature *Thirst* in 1949. In the Soviet Union realism was still officially socialist and usually heavy-going; it took the form of repetitive war films or biographical studies, seen at their best in Dovzhenko's *Michurin* (1947). The warm humanity that was to emerge more fully during the next decade could already be seen in Mark Donskoi's film *The Village Teacher* (1948).

In Britain, realism, as we have said, had already appeared

strongly in the war films; especially, to choose only outstanding examples, in Reed's *The Way Ahead* (1944) or Asquith's *The Way to the Stars* (1945). Its application to non-war subjects was more tentative; apart from Reed's films already mentioned, the years 1947–9 brought the Ealing productions *Hue and Cry, It Always Rains on Sunday, Scott of the Antarctic, Passport to Pimlico, Kind Hearts and Coronets* and *Whisky Galore*, the comedies among them light-heartedly, rather than fundamentally, realistic in treatment. To these should be added John and Roy Boulting's *Seven Days to Noon* (1947) and Michael Powell and Emeric Pressburger's *The Small Back Room* (1949). British realism remained tentative because at this stage it was not thought quite acceptable to present audiences with too exact a portrait of themselves; realism appeared as a rather original embellishment for light entertainment, fantasy or melodrama.

The 1950s, therefore, began with useful and sometimes exciting antecedents. During the following decade many film-makers were to appear who were capable of taking these new developments much farther.

The Way Ahead Britain 1944. Director Carol Reed
David Niven

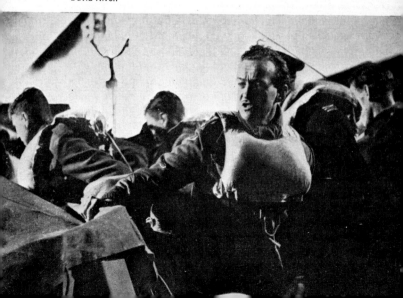

The Italian film

Film production in Italy dates from the earliest days of the cinema, when her reputation as the producer of spectacular films set in classical times, such as *Quo Vadis?* (1913) and *Cabiria* (1914), became established. Italian film history has little in it of distinction until the 1940s, but by then the industry had been built up for its prestige value by Mussolini, with the great Cinecitta studios, the largest at that time in Europe, and its celebrated training school, the Centro Sperimentale. It was during Mussolini's period that the international film festival was established in Venice. Most of the directors who were to become famous immediately after the war served their apprenticeship in conventional film-making before and during the war years.

Luchino Visconti was the first to break through the melting ice of fascism and produce a wholly realistic film of Italian life, in the teeth of authority. This was *Ossessione* (*Obsession* 1942), its story derived from the American writer James Cain's novel *The Postman always Rings Twice*. In spite of continual interference, Visconti (who came of a rich and aristocratic Milanese family, and had briefly worked as Jean Renoir's assistant in France before the war) managed to resist the pressures of censorship ('It was Mussolini himself who passed it,' claims Visconti of *Ossessione*) and finally screened the finished film in Rome in the form in which he had shot and edited it. 'It was like a bomb exploding in the cinema,' he has said. 'People saw a film which they had not thought possible.' It was considered that realism of this sort amounted to sedition. Subsequently this remarkable picture ran into further Italian censorship obstruction, and later into American copyright trouble, but in it lay the foundations of Italian post-war realism—the deep attachment to the vitality of working-class life, the uncompromising photography of Italian streets and highways (the direct opposite of the picturesque, tourist Italy), and the determination to show how poverty, over-crowding and sordid living-conditions affect the humanity of men, women and children alike. The acting concentrated on revealing details of behaviour, with nothing omitted which might add to the actuality of a scene or a character. 'Renoir helped me to understand that unless the cinema is nourished by a profoundly human idea, it is empty,' said Visconti in an interview some years later.

18

In spite of his aristocratic background, Visconti became associated with the political Left, a characteristic of many Italian realists, both writers and directors. Others, such as Rossellini and de Sica, were more vaguely liberal and humanitarian. Rossellini's *Rome, Open City* (1945), the film that first made Italian realism known throughout the world, emerged from the midnight discussions of a small group of resistance workers in Rome, during the period when the Allied advance was still taking place north of the city. Production began on borrowed money and with scratch equipment, and depended on the sheer devotion of the professional actors, actresses and technicians working on it. Using the absolute minimum of studio reconstruction, almost all the film was shot piecemeal on location, with many non-professionals in supporting parts. The actors and actresses drew directly on their experience of life in Rome under the Nazi occupation—the deprivations, the quick-witted actions of the resistance workers,

Ossessione Italy 1942. Director Luchino Visconti
Clara Calamai

Rome, Open City Italy 1945. Director Roberto Rossellini
Aldo Fabrizi, Anna Magnani

Sciuscia Italy 1946. Director Vittorio de Sica

the terrors and the absurdities of real life. The film saw the emergence of Anna Magnani as a star, through her extraordinary performance as Pina, the virago lover of the resistance leader. And a young writer called Federico Fellini assisted on the scenario.

While *Rome, Open City* (first shown in Britain during 1947) was astonishing the world and making the name of Rossellini almost amount to the rebirth of the cinema in Europe, de Sica (an actor already well-established with the Italian public, and the director of half a dozen sympathetic and unpretentious films) was making his first true realist picture, *Sciuscia* (*Shoeshine* 1946), about the distorted lives of the boys who existed as vagrants on the streets after the liberation, and became corrupted by being drawn into the black market. De Sica was to work closely from now on with the writer Cesare Zavattini, who had collaborated on the screenplay of *Sciuscia*, and who believed the cinema was so perfect a medium for the portrayal of real life, that the true screenplay could only emerge from the detailed follow-up of some actual event which reflected how the Italian people in the cities lived, felt and behaved. Although de Sica brought the knowledge of a professional actor to the direction of his film, he chose to use non-professional actors, though their voices were sometimes replaced by speech dubbed in afterwards by professional players.

While de Sica and Zavattini were working on *Sciuscia*, Rossellini and his writers, principally Sergio Amidei and Federico Fellini, had started on the production of *Paisa* (1945–6), a film made up of connected episodes which followed the path of war from the extreme south up to the valley of the Po in the north. The finest

Paisa Italy 1946. Director Roberto Rossellini

of these episodes was perhaps the last, with the snipers—Germans, Italian partisans, Allied soldiers—weaving their passage through the undergrowth and waterways of the marshes. Rossellini used a real corpse for the body of the dead partisan set afloat in the river with the crude notice 'Partigiano' stuck up over it. The grainy photography made the whole film seem to have been shot in some fearful twilight, and there was a rough improvisation in all the action that added to the pathos of the situation and the harsh bewilderment of this portrait of a war of attrition preying on the body of a country. The lonely landscapes of grass and water, the scattered shooting, the hasty interchange of signals and scraps of news, the child crying alone by the bodies of her family who had been shot for helping the partisans, are all unforgettable images of this desolate warfare.

These were the films which established neo-realism—to be followed soon by the war comedy *Vivere in Pace* (*To Live in Peace*), and by *Caccia Tragica* (*The Tragic Hunt*), *Sotto il Sole di Roma* (*Under the Roman Sun*), *Anni Difficili* (*The Difficult Years*), *Senza Pietà* (*Without Pity*), together with de Sica's celebrated *Bicycle Thieves* (1948) and Rossellini's *Amore* (1948), a two-part film in which he featured Anna Magnani first as a woman driven to distraction because she is being deserted by her lover, and then as a demented peasant who is casually seduced and then believes she is with child through some immaculate conception. This last story, called *The Miracle*, was scripted for Rossellini by Fellini, who also wrote *Senza Pietà* for Lattuada. Another screenwriter, Michelangelo Antonioni, had written *Caccia Tragica* for de Santis.

But most of these films, like so many of the initial productions of the liberated countries, repeatedly worked over the experiences of occupation and war. This subject had to be got out of their system, and in some countries, such as Poland and Yugoslavia, it is still unresolved and recurrent. The Italians, however, were among the first to sever themselves from war, and the initial phase of Italian realism rapidly turned to social problems and the pursuit of subjects reflecting the life of ordinary Italian people. *Bicycle Thieves* exposed the torture of chronic unemployment; Visconti's *La Terra Trema* (*Earth Trembles* 1948) showed the unsuccessful attempt by a Sicilian family of fisherfolk to own their boat, in a film which seemed at times an almost endless poetic study of impoverished Sicilian life; De Sica's *Umberto D* (1952) dwelt on the humiliations suffered by a respectable pensioner trying to

The Miracle (part 2 of **Amore**) Italy 1948. Director Roberto Rossellini
Anna Magnani (second from right)

La Terra Trema Italy 1948. Director Luchino Visconti

exist on utterly inadequate means. In each of these films there is no doubt of the director's sympathies. *Bicycle Thieves* has the most developed dramatic shape and the most developed sentiment in the relationship of father and son, while *Umberto D*, stressing the rather ignoble self-pity of the old man, is the most austere in its appeal to the sympathy of the audience. In *La Terra Trema* Visconti coaxed revealing performances out of the fishermen, whom he subsequently described as 'marvellously expressive' in their Sicilian dialect, which sounded at times, he thought, like the speeches of Sophocles. He found them quite unafraid of the camera and prepared to create their own dialogue under his guidance. In *Bicycle Thieves* the father was played by a mechanic from the Breda factory, while the child was a newsboy from Rome.

Bicycle Thieves Italy 1948. Director Vittorio de Sica

Umberto D Italy 1952. Director Vittorio de Sica
Carlo Battisti (right)

Il Tetto Italy 1956. Director Vittorio de Sica

Few of these films had much success with the Italian public. When the post-war recovery began to take effect, the film industry saw its opportunity to become one of the great centres of European production. What was left of the realist movement was at times diverted into comedy, and the era of the box-office prestige production began. Rossellini moved in other directions, and only de Sica tried to keep the tradition alive now and then—(for example, in *Il Tetto* 1956)—when he was free from his increasing commitments as an actor or director for more conventional films.

Hollywood-on-the-Tiber—production carried to the point of satiety or bankruptcy—service studios for wealthy, expatriate American producers—all this is a picture of the 1950s, with alternating booms and slumps, and a fierce drive to conquer world markets with Italian feature films produced in rising numbers that by 1961 exceeded 200 in the year. The previous year Italian films had for the first time earned more money in Italy than imported American films. The spectacular productions with which Italy had been traditionally associated were revived, in forms ranging from *Fabiola* to *Hercules conquers Atlantis*. M.G.M. made *Ben-Hur* in Rome with colossal settings. The industry suffered little from the competition of television until the 1960s. Films co-produced with France developed into a substantial part of Italian production—over one-third, for example, in 1961, each country sharing in the quota advantages of the other.

Certain large-scale producers began to emerge as dominating figures in Italian film-making, and became the sponsors of a new generation of directors. These producers were headed by Dino de Laurentiis, Goffredo Lombardo and Carlo Ponti. De Laurentiis represents the sophisticated tycoon. He became a producer at the age of twenty, after having worked as a film extra, an assistant director and studio manager. In the 1950s he produced deliberately for the international market (*Barabbas, War and Peace*—the latter co-produced with Carlo Ponti and the Americans) as well as for the home market (*Bitter Rice, La Strada*). In 1962 he began the first part of his production of *The Bible*, directed (after many alternative announcements) by John Huston, with a script by Christopher Fry. He believes in working on the grand scale and investing in high-cost production based on the English-speaking, not Italian-speaking, market. He has recently built his own massive studios on the Via Pontina.

Goffredo Lombardo took over his company, Titanus Films, from his father. He became, on the one hand, producer of *Sodom and Gomorrah,* and, on the other hand, of Visconti's later films, *Rocco and his Brothers* (1960) and *The Leopard* (1963). By 1964 Titanus, like much of the Italian film industry, was in financial difficulties after some years of over-production and inflated costs. Carlo Ponti, the famous husband of the famous Sophia Loren, like Dino de Laurentiis an astute businessman, co-produces with the Americans; his own films have included *Ulysses* and *Marriage— Italian Style.*

Among the massive output of conventional Italian films, there gradually emerged the work of a second generation of realists, directors whose imagination took them far beyond the conception of film-making represented by the earlier work of Rossellini and de Sica, or even the continued achievements of Visconti. Most prominent among them were the screenwriters Federico Fellini and Michelangelo Antonioni.

Fellini (born in 1920) began as a newspaper cartoonist and radio scriptwriter; he married the actress Giulietta Masina in 1943, and became a screenwriter after the war, working, as we have

The Leopard Italy 1963. Director Luchino Visconti
Burt Lancaster

La Strada Italy 1954. Director Federico Fellini
Anthony Quinn

seen, with Rossellini. This he has called 'a unique period of awakening'. After serving as an assistant director, he made his own first independent film, *I Vitelloni* (*The Drones*), which won him an award in 1953 at the Venice Film Festival. This success immediately led to other productions, including *La Strada* (1954) and *Notti di Cabiria* (1957), both featuring his wife in *tour de force* performances which fired the enthusiasm of the critics and public alike. Then followed the two films that made his work at once

La Dolce Vita Italy 1960. Director Federico Fellini

Notti di Cabiria Italy 1957. Director Federico Fellini
Giulietta Masina

La Dolce Vita Italy 1960. Director Federico Fellini
Anita Ekberg

8½ Italy 1962. Director Federico Fellini

highly controversial and world famous, *La Dolce Vita* (1960) and
8½ (1962). With these films he outpaced normal realism, and
entered the freer, fuller world of the creative imagination.

Fellini's work is far easier to describe than define. He is a compulsive film-maker, giving his intuition free play and letting his films develop through a form of free association of action and image. He has claimed that his films have a hand in their own creation, like Pirandello's *Six Characters in Search of an Author*. His father was a commercial traveller, and he spent his youth in the boring, bourgeois world of Rimini, to be seen in *I Vitelloni*. His education has made him anti-clerical rather than anti-religious. He is essentially a showman who indulges himself in public and enjoys being the *enfant terrible* who flusters the censors, while at the same time he retains a private, almost shyly retiring world of his own. He projects his personal experiences in images that constantly invade his films and lie at the root of $8\frac{1}{2}$, so called because it was his eighth actual production, plus the 'half' he contributed to the multiple film *Boccaccio '70*. In September 1964 he began work on his first film in colour, *Giulietta degli Spiriti*. *Giulietta of the Spirits* shows a woman's response to her life's experience and to her love for her unfaithful husband in the form of visions conjured up during spiritualistic seances.

Improvisation is essential to Fellini's work, but it is improvisation that results from a long gestation of every subject he undertakes. Whether or not he learnt the potentialities of improvisation from Rossellini (for whom such methods were frequently disastrous), for Fellini it means a free expansion of the subject, a kind of visual *cadenza*. Sometimes his imagery is striking rather than profound, like the sequence at the beginning of *La Dolce Vita* when the statue of Christ is flown by helicopter over Rome, to the delight of the gay girls sunbathing in bikinis on the rooftop. The touchy Italian censorship was affronted by this film, with its exposure of life among the rich, purposeless, indulgent segment of Roman society; the aristocracy was affronted; the Church was affronted. Fellini offended the political Left by refusing to support their idea that the film constituted a political attack on the Right. 'It does not set out to be controversial, or satiric or moralistic. It is a gay story intending only to amuse,' wrote Fellini when the film had just begun its release. 'It is the story of the life, the loves and the reportages of a journalist who has no moral scruples in his relationships.' Fellini does not want to be tied down to any fixed viewpoint.

In $8\frac{1}{2}$ he made his most personal work so far, the experiences of a film director, played by Marcello Mastroianni, who is under pressure from every side to make a film, but does not know what to create. The film is a fable of a man haunted by monsters in the

Il Grido Italy 1957. Director Michelangelo Antonioni

Le Amiche Italy 1955. Director Michelangelo Antonion

shape of all those non-creative people who plague him, the creative artist, while, in addition, the disturbing memories of his youth return like nightmares to increase his discomfort. The continuity of the action of the film, both real and illusory, is a projection of his experience. Fellini wonders why $8\frac{1}{2}$ has puzzled people; for him it shows exactly how any man in that difficult situation would see his life—part real, part unreal, part present part past.

Antonioni (born in 1912) has also developed into a highly creative, individualistic film-maker, after a period of screen-writing. He, too, had a provincial upbringing, in Ferrara. As early as 1942 he had assisted Marcel Carné on *Les Visiteurs du Soir*, and later directed documentaries, working at the same time as a film critic. His first feature film was *Cronaca di un Amore* (1950); his most celebrated films are *Le Amiche* (*The Girl-Friends* 1955), *Il Grido* (*The Cry* 1957), *L'Avventura* (*The Adventure* 1959), *La*

Le Amiche Italy 1955. Director Michelangelo Antonioni

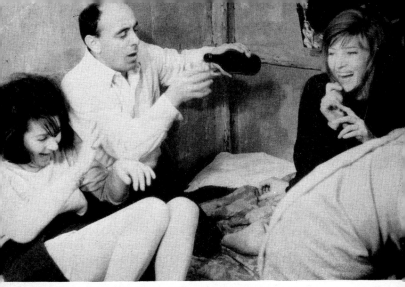

The Red Desert Italy 1964. Director Michelangelo Antonioni
Monica Vitti

Notte (*The Night* 1960), *L'Eclisse* (*The Eclipse* 1961) and *The Red Desert* (1964), in which Antonioni used colour photography experimentally to reflect a mentally disturbed woman's reactions to life with her husband and child in an overpoweringly industrialized environment. Since *L'Avventura* Monica Vitti has appeared in all his films and is closely associated with him; she had originally helped him with the dubbing for *Il Grido*.

Although in almost every respect Antonioni is the opposite of Fellini—'Fellini forces reality,' he has said, 'Visconti dramatizes reality; I try to *undramatize*'—they are alike in believing in the direct relationship of their work to the nature of the society and period in which they live. 'My films are in search of themes that are current, specific, burning,' wrote Antonioni in 1954. He, too, believes in improvisation in depth, using the inspiration of the actors' presence and the setting, as well as the active handling of the camera, to help him create the form of the shooting. He remains primarily his own screenwriter. His principal films, like Fellini's, have been variations on a highly personal theme, revealing his response to what he has observed, but not pointing any moral about it. Of *L'Avventura* he has said : 'I wanted to analyse the sentiments as they are today ; sentiments and emotions—loves, regrets, states of feeling—change, just as science and technology change. . . . I did not make the film to demonstrate a thesis. . . . I see my films as narratives, *romans par images*.' He wants his actors to *be*, not to perform, and as far as possible he films in the order of the story. 'In all my films I think I have eventually developed the same theme—the fragility of sentiments,' he says. '*La Notte* is the story of a married couple who suddenly, one day, discover that they no longer love each other. They are desperate about it, but what can they do?' Also: 'We live in an age where nothing is stable any more. Even physics have become metaphysical. Everything is changing. Why don't we like to admit that the psychology of people is also changing?'

The Red Desert Italy 1964. Director Michelangelo Antonioni
Monica Vitti

L'Avventura Italy 1959. Director Michelangelo Antonioni
Gabriele Ferzetti (second from right)

On pages 40/41
L'Eclisse Italy 1961. Director Michelangelo Antonioni
Monica Vitti, Alain Delon

Antonioni's films are virtually without plot; they present people passing through a key phase in their lives. They move in and out of love, living in a social milieu where they feel acutely the imbalance of their emotions—the island search for the lost girl who is never heard of again in *L'Avventura*, the midnight party in *La Notte*, the sequence in the strident stock exchange in *L'Eclisse*. Antonioni's players, even more than Fellini's, need to suggest states of mind rather than overtly project them. The best performances in Antonioni's films have come from Mastroianni, Monica Vitti, and Jeanne Moreau from France. Antonioni likes to excite instinctual, not intellectual performances from his players. His films are normally about love, or its rejection, yet he regards eroticism as a disease of our age, a kind of egocentric game played by the wealthy and over-indulged people whom he principally portrays. Like Fellini, he does not understand why his films are difficult for some audiences to follow, or frustrating because of the slowness of pace with which seemingly small events are observed.

L'Avventura was booed at the Cannes Film Festival. He has, he claims, 're-invented cinematic pace. The rhythm may be fast or slow,' he says, 'but it is the rhythm of life.'

In many respects his technique is opposed to the dynamic concept of cinema, while the technique of Fellini's work or of the films from the French *nouvelle vague* are in favour of the dynamic concept. He makes little use of camera or editing devices; he achieves his point through prolonged observation, seldom through sharp cutting. His films, therefore, have their detractors; there are some people who simply cannot stand them. Yet they are realistic in the fuller sense; they make *Bicycle Thieves* seem wholly theatrical and audience-conscious. They are rich and shapely, conveying a phase in human relationships and experience that can have no precise beginning or end, as in life itself.

La Notte Italy 1960. Director Michelangelo Antonioni
Marcello Mastroianni, Jeanne Moreau

Accattone Italy 1961. Director Pier Paolo Pasolini

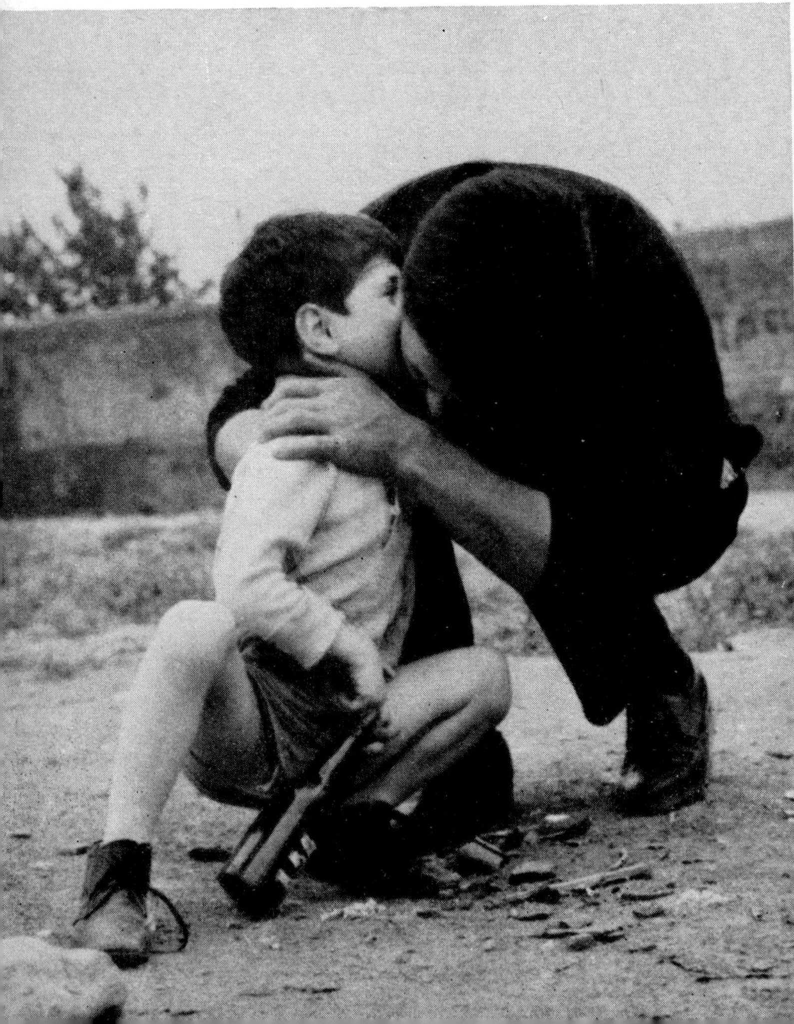

I Basilischi Italy 1963. Director Lina Wertmüller

Other Italian directors have produced films in the wake of the great achievements of Fellini and Antonioni. They include Pier Paolo Pasolini, with his *Accattone* (1961), *Mamma Roma* (1962) and *The Gospel according to Saint Matthew* (1964), Francesco Rosi with *Salvatore Giuliano* (1961), Giuseppe Patroni Griffi with *Il Mare* (1962), Ermanno Olmi with *Il Posto* (1961), *I Fidanzati* (*The Engagement* 1963) and Lina Wertmüller with *I Basilischi* (*The Lizards* 1963). Pasolini, a writer who is militantly to the

Il Mare Italy 1962. Director Giuseppe Patroni Griffi
Umberto Orsini, Françoise Prévost

Left in his politics, claims that the hero of *Accattone,* a young
delinquent, 'is struggling in the mud to save his soul', but that he
is saved not through his social or political consciousness, but
through love. *The Gospel according to Saint Matthew* is remarkable as a proletarian version of the story of Christ seen essentially
as a peasant-prophet. Griffi's *Il Mare* is an intense and stylized
portrait of three strangers in trouble. A man, a woman and a
youth meet on the deserted island of Capri in winter and try to
form relationships, which in each case fail.

Vaghe stelle dell'Orsa . . . Italy 1965. Director Luchino Visconti
Claudia Cardinale

Il Mare Italy 1962. Director Giuseppe Patroni Griffi
Umberto Orsini, Dino Mele

Il Posto Italy 1961. Director Ermanno Olmi
Sandro Panzeri, Loredana Detto

Olmi's films, which are concerned far less with social and psychological tensions, are now emerging as yet another form of realism, the amused, sympathetic, leisurely observation of normal human behaviour. *Il Posto*, the feature film that gave Olmi prominence in the Italian cinema after a lengthy career in documentary films, shows the opening phases in the career of a boy undertaking his first job in a firm that offers him what he is supposed to want most—a safe, unenterprising life, representing the ideal of respectability and security. In *I Fidanzati* Olmi carries the subtle art of the observer still farther in a study of the revival of a man's love for his too-familiar fiancée when he is separated from her while working in Sicily. Olmi's fluid, unemphatic technique is masterly in its rejection of any unnecessary stress or strain. Like Antonioni, he avoids the *fortissimo* of traditional drama.

I Fidanzati Italy 1963. Director Ermanno Olmi
Carlo Cabrini, Anna Canzi

These films, along with those of Fellini and Antonioni, have helped in the process of expanding, developing and maturing the European cinema. No other country has gone farther in this than Italy, though France has been more prolific, exuberant, youthful and febrile in technical experiment.

Giulietta degli Spiriti Italy 1965. Director Federico Fellini

Salvatore Giuliano Italy 1961. Director Francesco Rosi

The French film

The cinema has always been quick-moving. Reputations rapidly rise and fall; the critics seize on new trends in current work and pull new movements out of their hats. If Fellini and Antonioni are right when they claim to make their art out of their reaction to what immediately surrounds them, then their films, and the techniques they represent, may well begin to date in a decade or so. The films of Marcel Carné and Jacques Prévert made a quarter of a century ago appear utterly unrelated to us now, yet there was a time when the melancholy fatalism and character symbolism of *Quai des Brumes* (1938) and *Le Jour Se Lève* (1939) seemed as contemporary as the melancholy of Antonioni now; and the French film-makers prominent at the time (Clair, Cocteau, Vigo, Carné, Renoir principally) appeared in their various individual ways to be creating a revealing and poetic image of the period. But this was pre-war. Vigo died with only *Zéro de Conduite* (1933) and *L'Atalante* (1934) as his major films; Carné could only repeat himself during and after the war when the times were out of joint; while Clair continued to develop his own personal style of fantasy and elegant comedy in a post-war period seeking something radically different. Cocteau pursued his theatrical idiosyncrasies—most successfully of all in *Orphée* (1950). Only Renoir survived in a manner that still seemed wholly relevant; he kept

Opposite and below
Orphée France 1950. Director Jean Cocteau
Maria Casarès

himself free of the past, while his best pre-war films, such as *La Grande Illusion* (1937) and especially *Partie de Campagne* (1937) and *La Règle du Jeu* (1939) still made good sense in the 1950s and 1960s.

But the French never produced a neo-realist movement, only a number of realist films—for example, René Clément's film of resistance during the occupation, *La Bataille du Rail* (1946), Louis Daquin's left-wing *Le Point du Jour* (1948), Henri Clouzot's film of detection in the American manner, *Quai des Orfèvres* (1947), and his *Le Salaire de la Peur*, (*The Wages of Fear* 1953), Jacques Becker's *Antoine et Antoinette* (1947), *Edouard et Caroline* (1951) and *Casque d'Or* (1952), the last a study of con-

La Bataille du Rail France 1946. Director René Clément

Le Point du Jour France 1948. Director Louis Daquin

On pages 56/57
Manon France 1949. Director Henri-Georges Clouzot

flict between love and other loyalties in the Paris of 1900, with Simone Signoret; or that outstanding achievement of the immediate post-war years, Claude Autant-Lara's tragic study, with Gérard Philipe, of an adolescent boy's infatuation for a married woman, *Le Diable au Corps* (1947), adapted from Raymond Radiguet's story. The mannered beauty of the past, in the Carné–Prévert tradition, lingered on in the unexpectedly tender, fatalistic film that André Cayatte made from a script by Prévert, *Les Amants de Vérone* (1948). Carné himself made *Les Portes de la Nuit* (1946) as a last romantic stand in his series of symbolic dramas in which beauty is defeated by ugliness. The effects of the rising existentialist philosophy appeared in Delannoy's *Les Jeux Sont Faits*

55

Quai des Orfèvres France 1947. Director Henri-Georges Clouzot
Louis Jouvet (first on left)

Antoine et Antoinette France 1947. Director Jacques Becker

(1947), which Sartre himself scripted. Apart from them all stood that ultimate puritan of the cinema, Robert Bresson, with *Les Dames du Bois de Boulogne* (1944), and his first wholly individual film *Le Journal d'un Curé de Campagne* (1951), an ascetic portrait of obsessive conscience in a young Catholic priest suffering from a fatal disease.

Le Journal d'un Curé de Campagne France 1951. Director Robert Bresson
Claude Laydu, Nicole Maurey

Le Diable au Corps France 1947. Director Claude Autant-Lara
Gérard Philipe

The liberation of France did not relieve the country of political, economic or social distress. The moral dislocation brought about by the occupation could not simply be forgotten, and the French audience has always been a prickly one to entertain, seeking political significances to applaud or attack in the latest films. The *film noir*, often the film of despair, became a characteristic of the early post-war period, and many directors conformed: Yves Allegret with *Dedée d'Anvers* (1947) and *Une Si Jolie Petite Plage* (1948); Clouzot with *Manon* (1949); and, later on, Clément with *Les Jeux Interdits* (1952), a brilliant but morbid study of two children's preoccupation with death, and Zola's *Gervaise* (1956); and, finally, Clouzot with his horror film, *Les Diaboliques* (1954). André Cayatte, a lawyer by training, began his series of attacks on the French legal system with *Justice est Faite* (1950) revealing fallacies in the jury system, and *Nous Sommes Tous Des Assassins* (1952) which exposed the horrors of capital punishment—films described by the French critic, André Bazin, as 'a terrorism of reasoning' with 'the traumatic quality of a nightmare'. Meanwhile,

Les Jeux Interdits France 1952. Director Réne Clément

Justice Est Faite France 1950. Director André Cayatte

crime was paying at the box-office through French gangster films such as Dassin's *Rififi* (1955), and the new-style films of sex were initiated by Roger Vadim's *Et Dieu Créa la Femme* (1956), featuring the ineffable Brigitte Bardot, who had made a brief but marked appearance the previous year in the British comedy of sex *Doctor at Sea*.

The origin of the 'new wave' in the French cinema is complicated. On the surface it is the natural rebellion of a young and self-conscious generation of artists against the older generation, introducing a fresh approach to both subject and technique. But it is also many other things—the spectacular triumph of film theorists and critics turned film-makers and, deeper still, the protest of a whole section of the French against the particular experiences their nation was undergoing. Of one thing they were certain, they could not stand the work of the older generation, except for Renoir. Also, they idealized certain forms of film-making from abroad, especially the American films of which they had been starved during their adolescence—the Westerns and the gangster films. And they were the first generation young enough to be able to discover afresh the silent films and their techniques, instead of merely recalling them nostalgically as an experience in the past.

The French film industry, fortunately for the new-wave directors, is relatively individualistic in its structure—basically a matter of a large number of companies producing or co-producing films for cinemas free from the restrictions imposed by large-scale organization in chains or circuits. In 1952, after a period of crisis and recession, a new system of government financial aid for both shorts and features (in the form of advances to be repaid from profits) encouraged production which, in spite of the recurrent economic problems and perpetual battles with censorship, has kept feature production (and co-production, especially with Italy) at a level, normally, of some 100 to 150 films a year.

The new wave was to some degree anticipated through the making of shorts during the earlier 1950s. Georges Franju, one of the older generation (he was born in 1912), made *Le Sang des Bêtes* (1949), an objective, relentless study of animal life and death in a slaughterhouse; *Hôtel des Invalides* (1951), a subtle protest against the human slaughter of war worked into a patriotic film about the relics of war and war veterans; and *Le Grand Méliès* (1952), a tender, imaginative portrait of the dead film pioneer, impersonated by his son. Alain Resnais (born 1922) made *Van*

Le Grand Méliès France 1952. Director Georges Franju
Méliès is impersonated by his son

Gogh (1948), *Guernica* (1950), *Nuit et Brouillard* (1955), a film about the concentration camps, and *Toute la Mémoire du Monde* (1956). Jean-Luc Godard (born 1930), François Truffaut (born 1932) and Agnès Varda (born 1928) were among other new-wave directors who established themselves through short films. The new wave also reflected the common cause of the critics writing for the intellectual film journal, *Cahiers du Cinéma*. Truffaut, Godard, Claude Chabrol (born 1930) and Jacques Rivette (born 1928) were all critics for the *Cahiers* during the 1950s.

The feature films which first characterized the new wave were (apart from Vadim's *Et Dieu Créa la Femme*) : Alexandre Astruc's *Les Mauvaises Rencontres* (1955), Louis Malle's *Les Amants* and Chabrol's *Le Beau Serge* (both 1958), and, more directly, Truffaut's *Les Quatre Cents Coups,* Godard's *A Bout de Souffle* (*Breathless*) and Resnais's *Hiroshima, Mon Amour,* all released in 1959. It is well known that Chabrol financed his first feature by using money his wife had inherited ; Truffaut's film had been made on the most modest of budgets with the help of private investors and the monetary award he had received for his short film, *Les*

Mistons. The instant success of these films gave producers the idea that all that was needed was youth behind the cameras. The new wave was in business.

These films at once revealed freedom from convention. Vadim, a former journalist of Russian origin, presented his wife Brigitte Bardot in the part of the utterly emancipated, utterly sensual modern girl of *Et Dieu Créa la Femme*—the first appearance of the Bardot syndrome on which Simone de Beauvoir was to write her celebrated essay. This film managed to be at once simple and subtle in a way that comes close to the neo-realism of the Italians. In *Les Amants* Louis Malle told the story of a woman who leaves her husband and child for a lover she barely knows; with

Les Amants France 1958. Director Louis Malle
Jeanne Moreau, Alain Cuny

its intense love scenes filmed in close-shot and its deliberately unresolved characterization, the audience is forced to adopt some kind of individual attitude to the people in this film, as they would were the characters real. Astruc's film concerns a group of young intellectuals in a story involving an abortion; it caused some pretty brisk controversy.

But when both Truffaut's *Les Quatre Cents Coups* and Resnais's *Hiroshima, Mon Amour* won awards at the Cannes Film Festival in 1959, the movement was launched, and the term *la nouvelle vague* used by the press became general. Truffaut had experienced a reform school in his youth, and it was through the film critic André Bazin of the *Cahiers* that he had been brought into contact with films and become a critic. *Les Quatre Cents Coups*, the story of a misunderstood child driven to desperation, is an objective, painful but somehow generous observation of the narrow, bourgeois world which Truffaut knew too well. It was

Les Quatre Cents Coups France 1959. Director François Truffaut

filmed on location in Paris and elsewhere, and Truffaut has such sympathy in his handling of the child that the film has lyrical qualities in spite of its harshness. Truffaut takes no side; he leaves matters to sort themselves out in the minds of the audience. Of his method of work he said at the time: 'I work practically without a shooting-script; all I prepare is the dialogue. And when I have scenes too delicate to be shot in the usual way—like Antoine's scene with the psychologist—I clear everybody out and lock myself in alone with the actors and the cameraman. You can't put the best moments of a film down in a script.' Two years later, the period of *Jules et Jim*, it was the same. 'I start with a very imperfect script,' he said again, 'in which there are certain elements that please and stimulate me. Characters that strike some chord of response in me. A theme that lets me "talk about" something I want to film. As I work I find I am eliminating all the scenes of story transition and explanation. So it can happen that when the film is done, it is completely different from what it was proposed to say in the first place. The shooting of the film is that sort of adventure.'

Hiroshima, Mon Amour was very different. In his short film, *Nuit et Brouillard*, Resnais exposed the audience to the horrors of the concentration camps by avoiding any sensationalism or dramatic expression of horror. The film builds its emotion from the quiet accumulation of damning fact arising out of the images. In *Hiroshima, Mon Amour* (with a script by the novelist Marguerite Duras), Resnais shows the same passionate detachment, the cumulative effect that comes from an objective presentation of the terrible. There is considerable use of narration within the dialogue; it is an account of twenty-four hours in the life of a young French film actress, a married woman, who has been working on location in Hiroshima; she falls in love with a Japanese, who is also married, and their love-making and its aftermath before what seems their inevitable separation force her to relive in the arms of this understanding stranger a major experience in the past, when she was a girl of eighteen in love with a German soldier during the occupation of France. The soldier had been shot before her eyes on the very day her provincial town was liberated, while she had been shaven and forced to make a bitter penance in hiding for dishonouring her country. She needs to relive the experience in order to purge herself of both this loss of love and the bitterness which she still feels. The memories are seen against the background of the nuclear destruction of Hiroshima—the film opens with a long factual sequence on the explosion and its aftermath, interwoven with intimate scenes between the girl and her Japanese lover. The personal tragedy reflects the universal one, while the universal tragedy illuminates the personal one.

Hiroshima, Mon Amour has been the pivot for endless controversy, interpretation and comment; like many new wave films, it is without any overt or defined point of view with which the audience can comfortably agree or disagree. Even the comments made by the girl seem detached, withdrawn, allusive in their literary formality; the feeling of the characters is meticulously observed, while the action is crosscut from present to past, from immediate emotion to that recalled with such agonized bitterness. A further dimension is added to this emotion by the music's alternating sadness with gaiety. Resnais is a stern aesthetic disciplinarian, editing afterwards with scrupulous care.

Breathless, made by Godard, nominally in association with Chabrol and with a three-page script outline by Truffaut, was different yet again. The situation (there is no story in the old-fashioned sense) involves Michel (Jean-Paul Belmondo), a petty

Hiroshima Mon Amour France 1959. Director Alain Resnais
Emmanuele Riva, Eiji Okada

Hiroshima Mon Amour France 1959. Director Alain Resnais
Emmanuele Riva, Eiji Okada

gangster full of amoral bravado, who steals a car, kills a police-
patrol in cold blood, and returns to Paris where he is conducting
an egocentric love-affair with an American girl, Patricia (Jean
Seberg), a would-be intellectual and writer who sells papers on
the streets. In the end she betrays him to the police in order to be
rid of him, a fact he accepts with indifference as he dies under
fire from the police. The American gangster films, for which the
Cahiers group had professed their admiration, provide the framework for Godard's first feature, a work full of a significant though
pseudo-intellectualized posturing by the actors, who are said to
have improvised their dialogue under Godard's supervision while
the film was being made. *Breathless* displays an utterly nihilistic

On pages 72/73
A Bout de Souffle France 1959. Director Jean-Luc Godard
Jean-Paul Belmondo, Jean Seberg

attitude through the behaviour of the principal characters, whose attitude conforms to no generally accepted moral code. The film has a technical brilliance which is far more effective than its childish philosophy—the celebrated jump-cuts force the pace of the action, releasing it from any kind of conventional sequence structure likely to impose a logic on what is happening, because it is precisely this logic that Godard's artistic nihilism is out to destroy. The influence of silent film technique is seen in the iris fades, which also give the continuity a kind of freakish touch. The characters are pointedly unsympathetic in spite of Jean Seberg's natural charm, an asset which is deliberately discarded at the end of the film. Michel and Patricia stand for the absence of any constraint from either moral or emotional ties; their behaviour is the ultimate in irresponsibility. But they still enjoy their Mozart.

Chabrol's self-financed film *Le Beau Serge* completed this initial counterblast by the new wave during 1958–9. It was shot in winter in a a mountain village in the Massif Central, the birthplace of François, a sophisticated student, who returns after an absence of twelve years, only to become involved in the hopeless degrada-

A Bout de Souffle France 1959. Director Jean-Luc Godard
Jean-Paul Belmondo, Jean Seberg

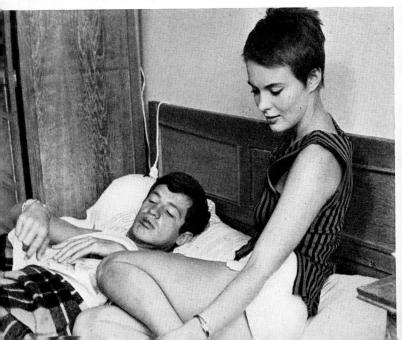

tion of the people he formerly knew. In the end he sacrifices himself to help redeem Serge, his childhood friend. Chabrol used a village in which he had himself spent some part of his childhood; the technique he employs is simple, economical, direct, almost documentary in its observation of place and people. The success of the film enabled him to draw on the French government's financial scheme to assist producers; he received about five-sixths of the costs of his next film, *Les Cousins* (1959), in the form of an official loan. *Les Cousins* showed the complex forms of corruption developed by a student group in Paris; Charles arrives from the provinces to begin his studies and to live with his cousin, Paul. He soon discovers that Paul and his friends practise promiscuity and advocate moral nihilism. Eventually, in a violent climax, Charles becomes the victim. Chabrol, in fact, appears to favour Paul, the nihilist. He indulges in various symbolisms in his presentation of the story, and also genuflects to Hitchcock. ('Hitchcock is one of the greatest inventors of forms in the history of the cinema,' he wrote in the *Cahiers*.) The result is a kind of amoral intellectual melodrama rather than a fully mature work.

Le Beau Serge France 1958. Director Claude Chabrol
Jean-Claude Brialy, Bernadette Lafont

Another film that was shown soon after, Jacques Rivette's *Paris Nous Appartient* (1958–60), caused a further flood of discussion, with violent opponents and adherents to its particular study of obsession. Ann, a student, innocent but enthusiastic, finds herself gradually drawn into a haunted world of half-defined political and artistic intrigue which in the end suggests that there is some cosmic conspiracy to bring about the destruction of mankind. The characters, including artists and political refugees, approach the symbolic in the variety of contemporary tensions they reflect. Ann, who represents normality, becomes so involved with them that she finally causes the man in love with her to commit suicide. This strange film, made mainly on location under great difficulties, and over an extended period of time, has a peculiar, hypnotic fascination, which is emphasized by the use of music in an eastern idiom, and wordless singing.

There was no question about the sensational effect these initial new wave films had on the critics and the more sophisticated public, and (through the film festivals) on the international status of the French cinema. The result was that *The Times* correspondent in Paris as early as March 1959 could write that 'today at least two-thirds of the interesting feature films recently completed or now in preparation are by directors unheard of three years ago, many of them still in their twenties'. The producers, drawing on their government loans, had plumped for youth. Fourteen months later, in May 1960, the news from Paris was that exhibitors were complaining that the excess of 'immoral' films was driving the public from the cinemas, and by October *The Times* correspondent was reporting on the pressures brought to bear on the French censors (the Film Control Commission of the Ministry of Information, representing primarily government departments and the film industry itself) to stop this depraving of youth by youth on the screen.

During the period 1959–63, around 170 directors in France made their first feature films (sixty-seven alone during 1959–60). This is surely a record in film history. The result was inevitable—a glut on the market, and a conglomeration of inexpert, pretentious, unscreenable celluloid, alongside a short list of striking and imaginative work. By 1964 Cannes, the cruellest of the festivals, was blasting the new wave it had launched with such enthusiasm five years earlier ; reputations recently considered golden were now represented as tarnished.

The new wave had never been a coherent or co-ordinated move-

Paris Nous Appartient France 1958–60. Director Jacques Rivette
Giani Esposito

ment, apart from the small circle of film-maker critics centred on
the *Cahiers*. Many directors, therefore, who found themselves
labelled new wave did not, in fact, regard themselves as being so,
and even those that were differed sharply from others associated
with the movement. The *Cahiers* group, as we have seen, had
developed their own cult of the American B-picture—enjoying
especially the formalization of violence, the melodramatic ele-
gance of the *film noir*. Directors such as Godard and Chabrol
consciously put form before content—the subject mattered little
provided a striking cinematic style was achieved. For Resnais, on
the other hand, with his marked literary interests, the subject was
an equal matter of concern. So it has been with Truffaut.

Once the modish elements in the new wave are allowed, the
stand the directors closely or loosely associated with the movement made for what came to be termed the *cinéma d'auteurs* and
camera-stylo has been of great importance. Alexandre Astruc, in

a now-famous article called 'Le Camera-Stylo' written as early as 1948, had claimed that a new age of the cinema was due to begin, in which the camera would create its own language, becoming the actual instrument of direct creation instead of a piece of equipment used to reflect something pre-prepared on paper. When the new wave film-makers talked of a *cinéma d'auteurs*, they implied a development in film-making which would lead to the creation of the subject by and through the use of the camera itself.

The 'free' photography, the improvisations in acting which verged on self-portrayal and personal appearance rather than performance, the arbitrary continuity with jump-cuts, the introduction of silent film techniques—all this became a characteristic of many new wave films. Soon new clichés of character were created—the young generation of students, pseudo-intellectuals, wastrels, petty gangsters and their girls, all living promiscuously and refusing to accept any form of responsibility for the conduct of their own lives or those of others. The only involvement was the rejection of involvement. But the original impetus behind what became the cliché remained valid—the break-up of the old-fashioned, artificial 'well-made' film about 'well-made' characters

Chronique d'un Été France 1961. Director Jean Rouch

Le Joli Mai France 1964. Director Chris Marker

and the emergence of a style of direction operating in free association with real-life characters, many of whom seemed to have
been met casually in the street.

The vocabulary and grammar of the conventional film were replaced by something new—either inspired or uninspired improvisation in which film-makers such as Jean Rouch experi-
mented in *Chronique d'un Eté* (1961), or, in the rarer cases, a new
academicism which (like the films of Resnais) challenged the
formal and obvious chronology as well as the subjects of the past.
In addition, the films associated particularly with Chris Marker
(*Cuba Si* 1961; *Le Joli Mai* 1963) introduced *ciné-vérité*, a
technique of film-making dependent on using the recently
developed lightweight equipment, allowing a greatly increased
mobility during filming with cameras that are either hand-held
or carried in a harness strapped to the chest of the cameraman,
together with the equally flexible recording of sound.

L'Année Dernière à Marienbad France 1961. Director Alain Resnais
Delphine Seyrig, Giorgio Albertazzi

Many films of interest and value have survived the new wave and the wreckage it produced. Resnais, perhaps the greatest single talent to have emerged from the movement, has produced *L'Année Dernière à Marienbad* (1961), the over-disputed film on the mystery of memory and identity written by Alain Robbe-Grillet, and *Muriel* (1963), a film in which once again the characters are forced to resolve the nature of their past commitments. Godard, in the school of disengagement, made *Le Petit Soldat* (1960), *Une Femme est une Femme* (1961), *Vivre sa Vie* (1962), *Les Carabiniers* (1963), *Une Femme Mariée* and *Bande à*

Muriel France 1963. Director Alain Resnais
Nita Klein

Vivre Sa Vie France 1962. Director Jean-Luc Godard
Anna Karina

Les Carabiniers France 1963. Director Jean-Luc Godard
Geneviève Galea (left), Catherine Ribero

Part (both 1964). Truffaut produced *Tirez sur le Pianiste* (1960), *Jules et Jim* (1961) and *La Peau Douce* (1964). Among the documentary pioneers of the new wave, Agnès Varda made her second feature in 1962—*Cleo de 5 à 7*, a hundred minutes in the life of a self-indulgent girl, a cabaret singer, while she waits for the results of a medical examination which may foretell her early death. Among the newcomers, Alain Jessua (one of those film-makers who does not regard himself as belonging to the new wave) has produced *La Vie à l'Envers* (1964), which with restraint, clarity and great humour shows how a young estate agent chooses to withdraw completely from the world in order to adopt a life of inner contemplation without any trace of mysticism.

Tirez sur le Pianiste France 1960. Director François Truffaut

La Peau Douce France 1964. Director François Truffaut
Jean Desailly, Françoise Dorléac

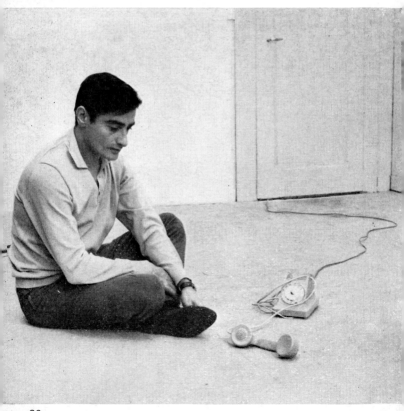

Le Caporal Epinglé France 1962. Director Jean Renoir

Un Condamné à Mort S'Est Echappé France 1956. Director Robert Bresson

Apart from the directors launched by the new wave, there are the individualists of the French cinema, Robert Bresson, Jean Renoir and Jacques Tati. Bresson shies away from any form of production which shows what he regards as the false emphasis of artificial drama. He works almost entirely with non-professional actors and actresses, whom he instructs to give utterly 'un-developed' performances, using voices as unstressed as possible in order to avoid artificial inflexions. In his later films, in particular *Un Condamné à Mort s'est Echappé* (1956), concerning a prison escape during the war, and *Procès de Jeanne d'Arc* (1961), in which sections of the contemporary records of the trial are used in the script, this approach was carried to an extreme that leaves the audience faced only with the director's close observation of the action, in which the actors perform merely as lay-figures.

Jean Renoir, the perpetually young veteran of the French cinema, enjoys a master's warm familiarity with his medium, which he uses with an ease that has ranged from calculated precision to gay improvisation. He has also shown great interest in television technique. Both *Le Déjeuner sur l'Herbe* (1959) and *Le Caporal Epinglé* (1962) owed much to improvisation and sheer high spirits:

Procès de Jeanne d'Arc France 1961. Director Robert Bresson

the first a form of lyrical fable aimed against an excessive technological and scientific organization of humanity, the second a subtly equivocal and comic picture of life in a prisoner-of-war camp and the complex forms of comradeship it generates. Renoir's career has spanned the whole development of modern French cinema, from the avant-garde movement of the 1920s to the new wave and television. His zest, his humanity, his magnificent pictorial sense in handling countryside locations, and his sheer love of film-making, rise above all the theoretical and technical disputations of the cults and the anarchy of thought which too often makes what seems new one year appear out-of-date the next.

Jacques Tati is a brilliant mime who has used the film to extend his art, though he has also occasionally appeared as an actor in films other than his own. His personal films have appeared at rare intervals: *Jour de Fête* (1949), *Les Vacances de Monsieur Hulot* (1953) and *Mon Oncle* (1958). In each he uses the medium with an unpretentious subtlety to observe the incautious antics of a central character who, although he changes with each film, shares a common inability to come to terms with the physical

Jour de Fête France 1949. Director Jacques Tati

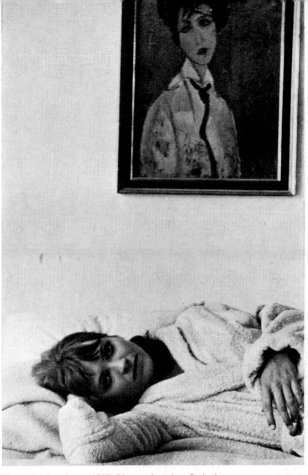

Pierrot le Fou France 1965. Director Jean-Luc Godard
Anna Karina

world, but gets in and out of difficulties with a balletic effrontery
which turns his special awkwardness into an act of spirited grace.
His timing is as expert as his wit; no one has moved on the screen
with the athletic assurance of the cycling postman of *Jour de Fête*
since Chaplin's youthful slapstick. Like most clowns, Tati is at
loggerheads with life, but survives with the masterly resilience of
a man whose cheerfulness defies defeat. His highly individual
and endearing humour was all the more welcome for first appearing during the harsh days of the *film noir*.

Ingmar Bergman

Bergman's very individual film-making, though recognizably Swedish with its lyrical pessimism, is unique in the Scandinavian cinema. Remarkable Scandinavian films had already appeared during the 1940s—for example, in Sweden Alf Sjöbeg's *Frenzy* (1944), a study of a pathological schoolmaster, and his later film *Miss Julie* (1951), a stylishly lyrical treatment of Strindberg's play, and in Denmark Carl Dreyer's *Day of Wrath* (1943), a morbid account of the clerical persecution of a witch in the seventeenth century, with its slow, stylized performances of studied, pious cruelty.

The script of *Frenzy* had been written by Bergman. Brought up in Lutheran piety and strictness, Bergman was to show a con-

Frenzy Sweden 1944. Director Alf Sjöbeg
Alf Kjellin

Miss Julie Sweden 1951. Director Alf Sjöbeg
Märta Dorff, Anita Björk, Ulf Palme

The Seventh Seal Sweden 1956. Director Ingmar Bergman
Max von Sydow (right)

Wild Strawberries Sweden 1957. Director Ingmar Bergman
Victor Sjöström

science-laden severity in his film-making. He was soon to dominate the Swedish cinema. He alternated film production with his work in the theatre, where he achieved his first success at the age of twenty-two with a production of *Macbeth* in 1940. Bergman began directing films in 1945, establishing himself as a creative director of exceptional poetic feeling with his earlier work, including his varied studies of lost love, *Summer Interlude* (1950), *Summer with Monika* (1952), and his sardonic comedy *Smiles of a Summer Night* (1955). A new strength and austerity appeared in his symbolist film of the circus *Sawdust and Tinsel* (1953) and in his stylized fable *The Seventh Seal* (1956), in which a medieval knight, torn by doubts, wins a brief interlude from Death, who comes to claim him.

By the age of forty-five, Bergman had made thirty films, written many scripts and produced around eighty plays. His later films include *Wild Strawberries* (1957), with a fine performance by Sjöström, the veteran actor-director, as the professor forced to relive his past life, *The Virgin Spring* (1959) and *The Silence* (1963). Bergman's themes, which often recur, are man's loss of faith, disillusionment and humiliation, and the nature of human relationships and their disintegration, especially between man and woman. Nevertheless, as these films so often show, we have a need for each other—'hell together is better than hell alone', the ultimate darkness is to be solitary. Though he is frequently lyrical,

The Virgin Spring Sweden 1959. Director Ingmar Bergman
above and below

delighting in the momentary release from his self-imprisonment, the philosophy behind Bergman's work remains deeply pessimistic. He has, however, a leaning for comedy, though this sometimes misfires, as in *Now About these Women* (1964). Throughout his later work his exact command over the performances given by the actors and actresses who constantly reappear in his films—such as Eva Dahlbeck, Harriet Andersson, Max von Sydow and Gunnar Björnstrand—and his controlled use of symbolistic imagery, reveal him as a great stylist of the cinema. Nevertheless, there is a certain theatricality in his approach, with his love of tension and visual shock. He has a weakness for expressionist melodrama, which links his films to the work of the Swedish and German expressionists of the 1920s, rather than to the more advanced work of the European cinema as a whole.

The Silence Sweden 1963. Director Ingmar Bergman
Gunnel Lindblom

Hue and Cry Britain 1947. Director Charles Crichton

The British film

British feature film-making has recently made a further move towards realism. Since the period when the best of the war films genuinely aimed to put people on the screen who were recognizably the same as the people in the auditorium, British features have tended to keep away from actuality, or merely to use it as a framework for something essentially non-realistic, such as the comic fantasies from Ealing Studios; for example, Charles Crichton's *Hue and Cry* (1947) or Alexander Mackendrick's *The Man in the White Suit* (1951), or the more striking and imaginative films of Carol Reed, *Odd Man Out* (1947), *The Fallen Idol* (1948) and *The Third Man* (1949), in which the realism gives verisimilitude to the unusual in dramas or melodramas of tension. There was also some attempt to bring actuality into the period film, in particuiar Charles Frend's *Scott of the Antarctic* (1948).

The Man in the White Suit Britain 1951. Director Alexander Mackendrick
Joan Greenwood, Cecil Parker, Roddy Hughes, Colin Gordon, Michael Gough

The Fallen Idol Britain 1948. Director Carol Reed
Michèle Morgan, Ralph Richardson

Odd Man Out Britain 1947 Director Carol Reed
James Mason, Fay Compton

The Third Man Britain 1949. Director Carol Reed
Joseph Cotten

It Always Rains on Sunday Britain 1947. Director Robert Hamer
Googie Withers

On pages 104/105
Nine Men Britain 1943. Director Harry Watt

The Way to the Stars Britain 1945. Director Anthony Asquith
Michael Redgrave

The thread of realism so strongly marked in the better wartime films such as *Nine Men, Next of Kin, The Way Ahead* and *The Way to the Stars* (to which should be added certain dramatized documentaries using non-professional actors, such as *Western Approaches* and *Fires were Started*), was carried forward by David Lean, with sentimental touches from Noel Coward's scripts, in *This Happy Breed* (1944) and *Brief Encounter* (1945).

Brief Encounter Britain 1945. Director David Lean
Celia Johnson

The Queen of Spades Britain 1948. Director Thorold Dickinson
Edith Evans, Yvonne Mitchell

Great Expectations Britain 1946. Director David Lean
Bernard Miles (right)

But after this Lean turned aside to make his magnificently stylized adaptations from Dickens, *Great Expectations* (1946) and *Oliver Twist* (1947). Effective stylization, rather than realism, became in fact characteristic of the best work in British film-making, whether in Thorold Dickinson's *The Queen of Spades* (1948), in Laurence Olivier's Shakespearean films, or in the polished work of Anthony Asquith, often much influenced by literature and the theatre, such as *The Browning Version* (1951), or his excellent and original

Hamlet Britain 1948. Director Laurence Olivier

Orders to Kill Britain 1958. Director Anthony Asquith
Paul Massie (right)

The Small Back Room Britain 1949. Directors Michael Powell and Emeric Pressburger
David Farrar, Anthony Bushell

Orders to Kill (1958). The post-war studies of war included some films with a lively surface realism about men in action—for example, Jack Lee's *The Wooden Horse* (1950), Michael Anderson's *The Dam-Busters* (1954), or the long episode of the dismantling of the trick-bomb in Michael Powell's *The Small Back Room* (1949). The same kind of uncomplicated realism also distinguished

The Wooden Horse Britain 1950. Director Jack Lee
Leo Genn, Bryan Forbes, David Tomlinson

Scott of the Antarctic Britain 1948. Director Charles Frend
Harold Warrender as Wilson

The Overlanders Britain 1947. Director Harry Watt
Made on location in Australia

the semi-documentary reconstructions of other courageous actions, such as those of the explorers in Charles Frend's *Scott of the Antarctic* (1948) and the Australian cattlemen in Harry Watt's *The Overlanders* (1946).

An interesting reconstruction of the evacuation of London when it is threatened by a madman in possession of an atomic bomb was attempted by the Boulting Brothers in *Seven Days to Noon* (1950). The roots of a less tidy and therefore more closely observed realism lay in a series of very modest films: e.g. Jill Craigie's *Blue Scar* (1948), Bernard Miles's *Chance of a Lifetime* (1950) and

Blue Scar Britain 1948. Director Jill Craigie
Emrys Williams

The Brave Don't Cry Britain 1952. Director Philip Leacock
John Rae, Jock McKay

Philip Leacock's *The Brave Don't Cry* (1952). Two of these concerned the life of coal-miners, and Bernard Miles's film was a relatively light-hearted story shot on location in a small factory in Gloucestershire. Though their achievement was small compared with that of the best of the Italian neo-realists, these films are the direct predecessors of the newer British realism of the late 1950s, which, like the British war films of the past and the films of the French new wave, had more immediate roots in shorts film-making than in the feature film. Some of these short films were partly financed by the British Film Institute's Experimental Film Fund, others were sponsored by industry. Among them were Karel Reisz's and Tony Richardson's *Momma Don't Allow* (1955), shot in the Wood Green Jazz Club, Lindsay Anderson's film of the workers at Covent Garden *Every Day Except Christmas* (1957) and Karel Reisz's *We are the Lambeth Boys* (1958), set largely in a successful boys' club in London. These short films established the reputations of their makers,* so that when the time came they could be regarded as sufficiently experienced to take on feature commitments.

After the ovation for Jack Clayton's film *Room at the Top* (1958), which was freely adapted from John Braine's novel about a ruthless young clerk whose only aim in life is to intrigue his way through to success and money, it was evident that the public was prepared to accept more outspoken films, and on occasion heroes who were unsympathetic and ruthless. *Room at the Top* remained essentially a theatrical film, in spite of the excellence of the acting by Simone Signoret, Laurence Harvey and Heather Sears. It was Karel Reisz's *Saturday Night and Sunday Morning* (1960),

* Tony Richardson had a successful career as a stage and television director before he made feature films; Lindsay Anderson also became a prominent stage director.

Room at the Top Britain 1958. Director Jack Clayton
Simone Signoret, Laurence Harvey (left)

adapted from Alan Sillitoe's novel of working-class life in Nottingham, that presented a realistic rather than a theatricalized picture of its subject. There was no neat storyline, no carefully balanced assortment of characters; the film dealt very directly with a crucial phase in the experience of a high-spirited and hard-working boy who has neither the conscious ambition nor the education to realize that he is in a dead-end job which makes little call on his innate ability, with the result that he spends his surplus energy and money on drunken exploits and getting a young married woman pregnant. The problem of seeking an abortion for her disillusions him, and at the same time leads him on the rebound into an engagement to a young girl who is more sure of her needs than he is of his. This film, with fine performances by Albert Finney, Rachel Roberts and Shirley Anne Field, and excellently used locations in Nottingham, was the nearest to true social realism that the British feature film had yet reached.

Saturday Night and Sunday Morning Britain 1960. Director Karel Reisz
Albert Finney

A Taste of Honey Britain 1961. Director Tony Richardson
Rita Tushingham, Paul Danquah

Its success led to a number of films of varying merit which were either genuinely realistic or gave a passable imitation of realism. All were adapted from successful novels or plays, for one of the great limitations of British film-making is its utter dependence on other media for borrowing subjects. Granted this lack of originality, the borrowed works have often been adapted with success. The best included Tony Richardson's *A Taste of Honey* (1961), adapted from Shelagh Delaney's play, and his *The Loneliness of the Long-Distance Runner* (1962, from Alan Sillitoe's story), John Schlesinger's *A Kind of Loving* (1962, from Stan Barstow's novel), his *Billy Liar* (1963, from a play by Keith Waterhouse and Willis Hall), Karel Reisz's *Morgan* (1966), and

The Loneliness of the Long-Distance Runner Britain 1962.
Director Tony Richardson
Tom Courtenay

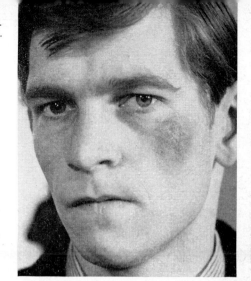

On Pages 120/121
A Kind of Loving Britain 1962.
Director John Schlesinger
Alan Bates, June Ritchie

Billy Liar Britain 1962. Director John Schlesinger
Tom Courtenay, Wilfred Pickles

Girl with Green Eyes Britain 1963. Director Desmond Davis
Rita Tushingham

Sidney Furie's *The Leather Boys* (1963, from a novel by Eliot George). In a style moving back somewhat towards theatrical comedy or drama were Sidney Gilliat's farcical comedy *Only Two Can Play* (1961, based on Kingsley Amis's novel *That Uncertain Feeling*), Jay Lewis's *Live Now, Pay Later* (1962), Desmond Davis's *Girl with Green Eyes* (1963) and Clive Donner's *Nothing but the Best* (1964).

The Leather Boys Britain 1963. Director Sidney Furie
Rita Tushingham, Colin Campbell

Moving away from direct realism was Clive Donner's fine, close adaptation of Harold Pinter's play *The Caretaker* (1963), shot in a rented house in a London suburb, and a number of British films directed by Americans—Stanley Kubrick's satiric fantasy, *Dr Strangelove; or, How I learned to Stop Worrying and Love the Bomb* (1963), Joseph Losey's science-fiction film, *The Damned*

The Caretaker Britain 1963. Director Clive Donner
Alan Bates, Donald Pleasence

Dr Strangelove, or, How I Learned to Stop Worrying and Love the Bomb
Britain 1963. Director Stanley Kubrick
Peter Sellers (centre)

(1961), and his film of psychological tension, in effect a symbolist film of innocence betrayed by evil, *The Servant* (1963), adapted from Robin Maugham's story of an utterly depraved manservant who obtains a hypnotic hold over his rich young master. Joseph Losey also adapted the play *King and Country* (1964) into a finely stylized production of theatrical intensity, with a touchingly intense performance by Tom Courtenay as a young soldier of the First World War on a desertion charge, which tests military law on an essential issue of humanity. With an original screenplay by the dramatist Robert Bolt, offering a highly critical interpretation of T. E. Lawrence, David Lean directed *Lawrence of Arabia* (1962) on magnificent locations mainly in Jordan and Spain; again this was a stylized film, using the characters to develop 'universal' themes, and Lawrence himself became a kind of symbolic, poetic figure of a great man subject to his own ambitious pride and autocratic vision of power.

The Damned Britain 1961. Director Joseph Losey

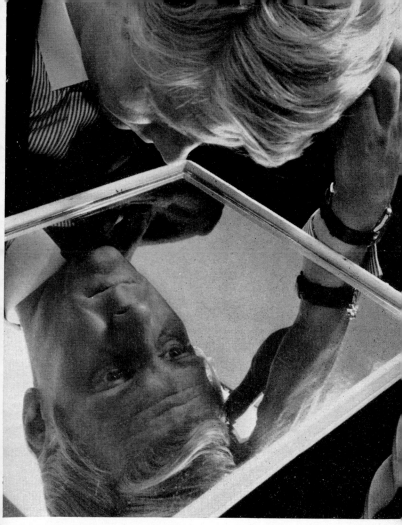

The Servant Britain 1963. Director Joseph Losey
James Fox

King and Country Britain 1964. Director Joseph Losey
Tom Courtenay, Dirk Bogarde

Lawrence of Arabia Britain 1962. Director David Lean
Peter O'Toole

This Sporting Life Britain 1962. Director Lindsay Anderson
Richard Harris, Rachel Roberts

Lindsay Anderson's film *This Sporting Life* (1962) was adapted from David Storey's novel about a miner of great physical strength who becomes a professional footballer in order to fulfil his need for self-identification and applause, and then fails because he is unable to sustain a love-affair with a young, equally disturbed widow. This film, in the direct tradition of realism, tried to enlarge the understanding of the leading character by holding a burning-glass up to nature. Like Fellini, Lindsay Anderson penetrates through the surface 'likeness' to explore inner motivation, enlarging nature in the process and developing actuality into metaphor, as in the violent, gladiatorial Rugby football sequence with which the film opens. Further than this, he uses split time, moving from the present action to the past, or to some other aspect of the present, with a continuity which is purely psychological. The film is a tragedy, with a climax when the woman dies that has some parallel with *La Strada*. In the tradition of heightened realism, it is the most advanced film that Britain has so far made.

This Sporting Life Britain 1962. Director Lindsay Anderson
Richard Harris

Reisz had not by 1965 followed *Saturday Night and Sunday Morning* with a film of equal vision. Tony Richardson, the most prolific producer in this form, has, especially in his production of *Tom Jones* (1963), drawn freely on the technical virtuosity associated with the French new wave, at times with an affectedness that hinders the film, as in *The Loneliness of the Long-Distance Runner,* when the wilful introduction of a succession of flashbacks slackens the tension of a climax which has been otherwise carefully constructed. John Schlesinger, whose previous career was primarily in television documentary films, has revealed that a new and resourceful imagination is developing in British feature film-making. Schlesinger has a sharp eye for the effective use of realism in ways which are at once witty and quick. In *Nothing but the Best,* a well-observed satiric film which is in theme not unlike *Room at the Top,* Clive Donner accepted a melodramatic turn in the plot at the end which detracted from the total value of the film. Sidney Furie, in *The Leather Boys,* allowed a considerable latitude of improvisation in the dialogue (deviating verbally from a pre-existing script), but on the whole British directors, unlike

Tom Jones Britain 1963. Director Tony Richardson
Albert Finney, Joyce Redman

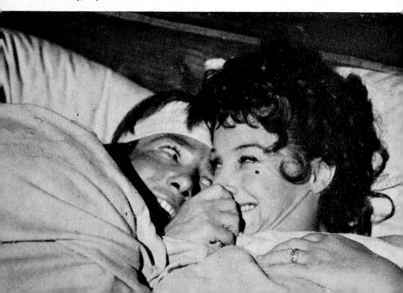

Lord of the Flies Britain 1961–3. Director Peter Brook

the French, prefer to leave little to chance and behave with exemplary if sometimes unimaginative self-discipline. An exception is Peter Brook's extraordinary adaptation of William Golding's *Lord of the Flies* (1961–3), shot with a cast of non-professional boy players on location in the Caribbean and drawing considerably on improvised action.

In Dick Lester's light-hearted films featuring the Beatles, *A Hard Day's Night* (1964) and *Help!*, and in *The Knack* (1965) which was developed from a play by Ann Jellicoe into a fantasy deriding fashionable obsessions with sex, the lightning continuity and free-wheeling improvisation associated with the work of such film-makers as Godard have dispelled the staid technique normally associated with British films.

The great lack in Britain is more fully creative film-makers in the way that Fellini, Antonioni or Truffaut are fully creative. Even the best British films are, as we have seen, normally derivative from other sources and lack, therefore, the final strength of imagination which can only come from an *auteur du cinéma* in the best sense of the term. Even if such a director should emerge, it is doubtful if he would be made very welcome by the distributors and exhibitors through whose hands his work must inevitably pass.

133

Darling Britain 1965.
Director John Schlesinger
Julie Christie

The Knack Britain 1965.
Director Richard Lester

The Soviet film

Soviet Russia, as the principal centre of film-making in the USSR since 1919, has endeavoured to set the pace for film production in the communist countries, all of which nationalized their industries after the war. More recently, during the period of the Khruschev régime, one sensed the impatience of the various national industries to develop their own independent, though still communist, film-making, more particularly in the case of those countries, such

The Cranes are Flying USSR 1957. Director Mikhail Kalatozov
Tatyana Samoilova

The Village Teacher USSR 1947. Director Mark Donskoi
Vera Maretskaya

On pages 136/137
War and Peace USSR 1965. Director Sergei Bondarchuk

as Poland, Hungary and Czechoslovakia, which had industries before the war, and therefore surviving technicians who wanted, once peace had returned, to continue making films.

In the Soviet Union as a whole, in spite of television (which only began to be fully developed after 1957), there are vast audiences recorded for the cinema, in the neighbourhood of eighty million a week in 1964. In any case, plans for television are integrated with those for the cinema. The various republics have their own feature film studios, and the total production in the Soviet Union is now some 150 feature films a year, of which about one-third come from the Moscow and Leningrad studios.

Individual studios, such as Mosfilm of Moscow or Lenfilm of Leningrad, control their own output, subject until 1963 to overall supervision by the Ministry of Culture and, since 1963, by a special State Committee. Film-makers in the Soviet Union are far more secure economically than their colleagues in the West, but it is difficult to see how they could ever make a film of which the authorities actively disapproved.

Production had come almost to a halt in the final years of Stalin's régime. A few so-called prestige films were made, all carefully designed either to glorify Stalin himself (*The Vow, The Fall of Berlin, The Battle of Stalingrad*) or to make some predetermined social point, like Donskoi's *The Village Teacher* (1947), an excellent and sympathetic portrait of a girl who brings education under the hardest conditions to a village in Siberia, or

Dovzhenko's stolid but human biography of the biologist Michurin (1948). With the change of régime in 1953 expansion started, and a newer, and in the end more liberal, policy of production began in Russia and the constituent republics. The result was a widening out of subjects, many having little or no direct propaganda or social message, and a deepening realization of individual as distinct from social problems—films such as the young director Grigori Chukhrai's *The Forty-first* (1956), in which a woman's love for a man under arrest by her as an enemy of the state is the principal theme, and Mikhail Kalatozov's *The Cranes are Flying* (1957), a sensitive study of a girl in love. Literary classics were adapted—notably, Sergei Youtkevich's colour film of *Othello* (1955), Grigori Kozintsev's version of *Don Quixote* (1957), Sergei Gerasimov's massive trilogy based on Sholokhov's *Quiet Flows the Don* (1957), and Joseph Heifitz's tender, nostalgic adaptation of the story by Chekhov, *Lady with the Little Dog* (1960). Later, Kozintsev was to make *Hamlet* (1963), possibly the finest Shakespearean film yet made, using Pasternak's prose translation.

The first sections of *War and Peace*, perhaps the most ambitious, beautiful and exact transposition of literature to the screen yet

The Forty-First USSR 1956. Director Grigori Chukhrai
Isolda Izvitskaya, Oleg Strizhenov

Othello USSR 1955. Director Sergei Youtkevich
Sergei Bondarchuk as Othello

Quiet Flows the Don USSR 1957. Director Sergei Gerasimov
Elina Bystrikskaya, Pyotr Glebov

Lady with the Little Dog USSR 1960. Director Joseph Heifitz
Ya Savina, Alexei Batalov

Hamlet USSR 1963. Director Grigori Kozintsev
Innokenti Smoktunovsky as Hamlet

Clear Sky USSR 1961. Director Grigori Chukhrai
Eugene Urbansky, Nina Drobisheva

Destiny of a Man USSR 1959. Director Sergei Bondarchuk
Sergei Bondarchuk

undertaken, were finished by the actor–director Sergei Bondarchuk in 1965; the complete film will probably last some eight hours.

Socialist films, with their message often strongly expressed in heroic speeches, are still, of course, produced—the widescreen production of *The Turbulent Years* (1960), which Dovzhenko's widow, Yulia Solntseva, directed from her husband's script, showed this, with its massively choreographed war scenes. But the emphasis in these socialist films was increasingly on individual problems; this was seen in the first film to be directed by the actor Sergei Bondorchuk, *Destiny of a Man* (1959), which is about the gradual recovery of a Russian prisoner-of-war through his love for a child, and in Chukhrai's *Clear Sky* (1961), the first film openly to rejoice at the passing of Stalin.

In Marlen Kutsev's film *I'm Twenty* (1965), a much freer technique of camera-observation has been introduced by a new, young director in a film revealing some of the uncertainties experienced by modern youth in the Soviet Union.

I'm Twenty USSR 1965. Director Marlen Kutsev

The Polish film

With the eye of authority fixed firmly on the screen, it is virtually impossible for the directors of Soviet feature films to use the cinema for any form of individual, personal expression, even if any of them might wish to do so. For this we must turn to Poland. Of all the communist film-makers, the small Polish group have shown since the 1950s the most marked independence. They have refused to be lined up for inspection. They had to start from nothing, in a country torn apart by the war and the subsequent social revolution. They represent a proud, edgy, nervous, romantic people, holding their own against a long and deeply troubled history as well as a current period which has been beset by difficulties, political, social and economic. They live in border territory, lying between the East–West factions and, as their films reveal, they are very responsive to Western culture. Discussion is free and fervent; the advanced films of the West are eagerly studied and ruthlessly criticized, along with other importations from the West, from books to jazz. Unlike the Russians, they have used the film to precipitate, and perhaps alleviate, their unease, as well as their more active emotions. As a result, they have made some of the best films that have appeared in Europe since the war.

Five Boys of Barska Street Poland 1954.   Director Alexander Ford

The Last Stage Poland 1948. Director Wanda Jacobowska

From 1950–5, Poland produced a total of only eighteen feature films. Their average annual production is now around thirty. Among the first post-war films to appear was Wanda Jacobowska's *The Last Stage* (1948), a restrained, courageous reconstruction of life in the concentration camp at Auschwitz made by a pre-war film-maker, who had herself been a prisoner. Another film by an established director was Alexander Ford's *Five Boys of Barska Street* (1954), dealing in realistic terms with displaced youth in Warsaw.

Ashes and Diamonds Poland 1958. Director Andrzej Wajda
Zbigniew Cybulski (left)

In 1956, round the time Gomulka came to power, film production was decentralized and several units were created of like-minded young film-makers working in each case under the general guidance of a senior director, such as Alexander Ford. Each unit, which carries its own individual name, such as Kadr, Start and Kamera, receives government finance for the work it is ready to do, but has remained, at least until 1965, quite independent of any orders from above as regards the subjects chosen for production. Polish films, therefore, are films of intuition and ideas, not propaganda. The celebrated film school at Lodz under its enlightened principal, Jerzy Toeplitz, works in direct association with the industry, and gave Andrzej Wajda (born 1926), Andrzej Munk (1921–61), Jerzy Kawalerowicz (born 1922) and Roman Polanski (born 1933), among others, their initial training. It was founded in 1947.

It was this system that permitted Wajda, after completing his training at the film school, to direct *A Generation* (1954), a study of youthful members of the resistance during the occupation, and to make it entirely in his own manner. Ford at that time acted as his mentor. Wajda works with the Kadr Unit; his first connection with the arts was painting. He approaches film-making as a romantic, intuitive observer of the flaws, ironies and beauties in human nature. Obsessed by the subject of war, he followed *A Generation* with *Kanal* (1957), in which another youthful resistance group during the 1944 uprising is hunted through the sewers of Warsaw, and *Ashes and Diamonds* (1958), which faces the moral issue of political assassination.

Kanal Poland 1957. Director Andrzej Wajda

The developing characteristic in Wajda's style has been described as baroque. Certainly his style changed from the quieter, more acceptably obvious realism of *A Generation*, which still half belongs to the first, brief, more conventional phase of post-war Polish cinema, to the more restless, more mannered, more personally exploratory style of *Ashes and Diamonds*. Wajda in his early thirties, like others of his generation who had endured their adolescence under the occupation, attempted in his films to face experiences that were still painful and unresolved. In *A Generation* the various young people dedicated to resistance in Warsaw during 1942 try to resolve these problems by joining in a common struggle against the Nazis; every character is alive and well observed, and never idealized in heroic terms. In *Kanal* the survivors of the resistance unit (whom we know from the start to be doomed) are again seen as individuals; they are characterized with affection, but already Wajda is beginning to show a certain technical virtuosity and even symbolism in his style. In *Ashes and Diamonds*

Innocent Sorcerers Poland 1960. Director Andrzej Wajda
Krystyna Stypalkowska

148

(like *A Generation*, derived from a novel), Wajda reaches the immediate post-war years to show the indecision of a young man (Zbigniew Cybulski with his symbolic dark glasses) who is involved with a right-wing group in the provinces and ordered to kill a communist leader. He can find no place for himself in a divided and desperate world during this period of political transition. Disillusioned and anxious only to get away from it all and make love to his girl, he finally kills his victim and is then himself killed by a passing patrol. Both deaths are needless, and the end is a bitter and ironic comment on the violence of the past. Cybulski (born 1927), who had also appeared in *A Generation*, is a well-known stage actor and producer; he gave a nervous, somewhat self-conscious performance as the hero, Maciek. The film is full of cinematic effects, often brilliant like those of Fellini, but sometimes over-calculated or melodramatic, like the chapel door being knocked open by the falling corpse after the mistaken killing at the beginning of the film and the symbolic use later of the crucifix suspended upside-down. Maciek was to become a symbol of the Polish anti-hero.

Of Wajda's later films, *Innocent Sorcerers* (1960) reveals Western influences the most, particularly those of the French new wave. This shows the young, sophisticated set in Warsaw, with their jazz clubs and bored attempts at casual sex. The action centres on a doctor and a girl who is a stranger to him. She spends the night in his room after being stranded in Warsaw; the game of seduction that they agree to play gradually breaks down as they begin to realize that they can care for each other as fellow human beings. Apart from the would-be happy ending (said to have been imposed on Wajda), this intimate film is sensitively unsentimental in its charm and touching because of the desire it shows in young people to escape from the rigorous limitations of their surroundings into the illusory glamour of the West. But the film was openly condemned by Gomulka for its lack of socialist realism at the Party Congress in July 1963. He also mentioned Polanski's *Knife in the Water* (1962), a film by a new director in his twenties in which, with detached irony, he observes every detail in the jealous gyrations of a husband and wife and a stranger, a young student; they invite him to join them for the weekend on their sailing boat and he provokes the worst elements of egotism in their characters, particularly in that of the husband. Polanski had already attracted attention with a provocative, almost surrealist short film *Two Men and a Wardrobe* (1958).

Knife in the Water Poland 1962.
Director Roman Polanski
Zygmunt Malanowicz, Jolanta Umecka

Salto Poland 1965.
Director Tadeusz Konwicki
Zbigniew Cybulski

If Wajda is romantic and subjective in his use of the cinema, Munk, who was also a member of the Kadr Unit, was the intellectual, the analyst. In *Eroica* (1957) he analysed, even denigrated, the myth of the hero in wartime in two complementary stories, the first about a petty swindler who, more by chance than conviction, becomes an unwilling volunteer in the Warsaw uprising, though in the end he seems to realize the necessity for resistance. The second story satirized life in a German prison camp, where the Polish prisoners' morale is kept going by the legend of a single bold escape by a man who is still in fact hiding in the camp, sustained by the few who know this dishonourable secret. This antiheroic film has the same scriptwriter (Jerzy Stephan Stawinski) as Wajda's *Kanal*. In *The Passenger* (1961; completed by Witold Lesiewicz, 1963), the film on which Munk was working when he was killed in a car-crash, he showed the problem of a German, Lisa, who is forced by a chance encounter long after the war with Marta, a Polish woman, to recall their relationship when Lisa was an overseer at Auschwitz and Marta a prisoner. *The Passenger*, a deep nightmare for all its restraint, is the most explicit film yet made about the psychology of the relationship of overseer and prisoner in the Nazi death-camps.

150

Eroica Poland 1957. Director Andrzej Munk

On pages 152/153
Electra Greece 1961. Director Michael Cacoyannis
Irene Papas (right)

The Passenger Poland 1961–3. Director Andrzej Munk and Witold Lesiewicz

With the later work of Jerzy Kawalerowicz, who became artistic director of the Kadr Unit in 1955, we leave this pre-occupation with the war period. *Night Train* (1959) was a stylishly directed thriller, Hitchcock—Polish, while *Mother Joan of the Angels* (1961) presented the story of the erotic obsessions of the demoniac nuns of Loudon in seventeenth-century France (adapted from a Polish novel about the incident, and not from Aldous Huxley's *The Devils of Loudon*, which was the basis for John Whiting's play on the same subject, *The Devils*). This, too, was brilliantly filmed, although ambiguous in its psychological and religious interpretation.

'Our cinematography,' said Gomulka at the 1963 Congress, 'cannot be an instrument used entirely for experimental purposes by a small group of artists.' He criticized Polish cinema for its lack of ideological content. Perhaps conventional Polish cinema had become too much concerned with the adulteries so dear to the bourgeois entertainments of the West, but this would not justify the loss of work undertaken in an atmosphere of freedom by established directors such as Wajda or talented newcomers like Polanski. Poland in barely ten years had created a small film industry, the best work of which had won the admiration of the world and gained awards at many of the film festivals. But political leaders in both the East and the West prefer the arts to present subjects which are generalized and expedient rather than individual and analytical or ironic. The restraints imposed one year may however disappear for a while during the next. The Polish directors are a resilient and resourceful group, and most of them have youth on their side.

Mother Joan of the Angels Poland 1961. Jerzy Kawalerowicz

Conclusion

At no period in its development has the cinema been more alive
and interesting than during the period 1950–65. To find any
parallel in the growth of invention and imagination we would
have to return to the period between *Birth of a Nation* (1915) and
the close of the silent period 1928–9, a mere fourteen years later,
the period that saw the film leave its swaddling clothes and develop
the mature art of such directors as Griffith, von Stroheim, Mack
Sennett, Chaplin, Keaton, Clair, Pabst, Flaherty, Eisenstein,
Pudovkin and Dovzhenko, as well as the experimentation of the
French avant-garde.

Now, as then, the film moves forward on a common international
front, with first one country, then another enabling individual
directors, or groups of directors, to develop their art. The countries
selected here have been in the forefront during the post-war
period in the European cinema. But film-makers elsewhere have
also contributed—for example, Michael Cacoyannis in Greece
(*Windfall in Athens* 1953; *Stella* 1954; *A Girl in Black* 1956;
Electra 1961), Juan-Antonio Bardem in Spain (*Death of a
Cyclist* 1955; *Calle Major* 1956), R. A. Stemmle (*Berliner
Ballade* 1949) and Wolfgang Staudte in Germany (*The Murderers
are Amongst Us* 1946; *Roses for the Prosecutor* 1959), Jiri
Weiss in Czechoslovakia (*Stolen Frontiers* 1947). Luis Buñuel,
who normally works in Mexico, exposed the false assumptions
of piety in his anti-Catholic film, *Viridiana* (1961), made under the
nose of the Spanish censorship.

Stolen Frontiers Czechoslovakia 1947. Director Jiří Weiss

The Shop on the High Street Czechoslovakia 1965.
Directors Ján Kadár and Elmar Klos

Diamonds of the Night Czechoslovakia 1964. Director Ján Němec

A Girl in Black Greece 1956. Director Michael Cacoyannis
Georges Foundas

The Loves of a Blonde Czechoslovakia 1965. Director Milos Forman

Viridiana Spain 1961. Director Luis Buñuel
Silvia Pinal

During 1965 we learnt of the significant progress that the younger generation of Czech film-makers had achieved. The ironic tragedy *The Shop on the High Street* (1964), directed by Ján Kadár and Elmar Klos, showed what anti-Semitism could mean in individual, human terms in a small town of German-occupied Slovakia; *Diamonds of the Night* (1964), director Ján Němec, used Jaroslav Kučera's *ciné vérité* photography to observe with great objectivity the reactions of two boys escaping from a Nazi concentration camp convoy to work their way through a hostile countryside, their minds haunted by visions of their life at home; *Joseph Kilian* (1964), a short feature directed by Pavel Juráček and Jan Schmidt, went even further in its allusive, hallucinatory treatment to reveal the insecurity of a young man who feels estranged from the society in which he lives. Milos Forman's charming, informal films, *Peter and Pavla* (1964) and *The Loves of a Blonde* (1965), have thrown new light on the more intimate lives of young people in Czechoslovakia.

Having advanced so far, we can only hope the European cinema will be able to sustain and develop its advances. There have proved to be adequate audiences in the world as a whole to support the advanced work of a Resnais, an Antonioni, a Fellini. But no director can go farther than the public is ready to follow. No public, no film. The cinema, more than all the arts, cannot survive in a vacuum. Our hopes, therefore, must extend to the public as well as to the film-makers. They advance together.

Joseph Kilian Czechoslovakia 1964. Director Pavel Juráček and Jan Schmidt

Index of Directors (*Italicized numerals indicate illustrations*)